Shadowed Dreams

Shadowed Dreams

~~~~~~~~~~

WOMEN'S POETRY OF THE HARLEM RENAISSANCE

Edited and with an Introduction by

Maureen Honey

Rutgers University Press
New Brunswick and London

Library of Congress Cataloging-in-Publication Data
Shadowed dreams : women's poetry of the Harlem Renaissance / edited and
with an introduction by Maureen Honey.
    p.   cm.
Bibliography: p.
ISBN 0-8135-1419-3 (cloth)   ISBN 0-8135-1420-7 (pbk.)
    1. American poetry—Afro-American authors.   2. American poetry—
New York (N.Y.)   3. American poetry—Women authors.   4. American
poetry—20th century.   5. Afro-American women—Poetry.   6. Harlem
Renaissance.   7. Women—Poetry.   I. Honey, Maureen, 1945–   .
PS591.N4S54   1989
811'.52'0809287—dc19   88-36972
                                                                    CIP

British Cataloging-in-Publication information available

TO THE MEMORY OF MAE V. COWDERY

Contents

Foreword

In the late 1960s and early 1970s, with the exciting rediscovery of figures like Countée Cullen, Jean Toomer, Langston Hughes, and Richard Wright (to name a few of the most well known), many young black women writers and scholars wondered aloud, at first mostly among themselves, and then to the larger world: "Where were the women who put pen to paper and gave voice to their creative impulses?" Of course, almost everyone knew of Gwendolyn Brooks, the first black poet to receive a Pulitzer Prize, and radical contemporaries like June Jordan, Carolyn Rodgers, Nikki Giovanni, and Sonia Sanchez who made impolite and even outrageous claims for blackness, on paper, on streetcorners, in local bars, and in demonstrations on college campuses and elsewhere, and they called themselves poets. But for most of us then, if there was an identifiable tradition in Afro-American literature, it was a man's world. Some of us, even as we ventured out to search for black female literary models, consoled ourselves with the idea that the women had been too busy keeping the "race" alive over its three-hundred-year-old American history to have found the time to write. Now we know that was not so.

Given such an inauspicious beginning to the search for black women writers, however, the pioneers who excavated the rich mine of which we are now aware—the tradition of black women writing in America—richly deserve all the credit we can give them. And as the thirty-one volumes (with one more to come) of the recent Schomburg Library of Nineteenth-Century Black Women Writers reveals, in spite of how difficult it must have been, black women wrote prolificly in all of the most popular forms—poetry, novels, short fiction, and autobiography. The first task was discovering the tradition; the second, and equally challenging, has been making the materials available to students and teachers.

Maureen Honey's fine volume, *Shadowed Dreams: Women's Poetry of the Harlem Renaissance*, makes a strong response to that second challenge. Although scholarship on the Renaissance has burgeoned in recent years, work on women remains to be done. At the same time, most of what has already been published on women writers, including on those who wrote during the Renaissance, has been on the novelists. Work in other fields lags behind. Consequently, *Shadowed Dreams* will occupy a significant place in the body of recovered Afro-American women's poetry, one equal to that of Erlene Stetson's 1980 landmark anthology, *Black Sister: Poetry by Black American Women, 1746–1980*. In addition, *Shadowed Dreams* comes at a most propitious time, following on the heels of Gloria Hull's *Color, Sex, and Poetry: Three Women Writers of the Harlem Renaissance* (1987), a text that focuses close attention on the lives and writings of a select group of women poets of that era. Both Stetson's and Hull's works set the stage for Honey's book, which gives a comprehensive view of the poetic achievements of the most important women poets of the period. This is the first time that anyone has attempted to do such a study of Harlem Renaissance women writers. Because of its timeliness, the text will be of immense interest to everyone interested in the Renaissance, offering a splendid resource for both general readers and those doing research on women in the Renaissance and black women poets in general.

Shadowed Dreams contains the work of a number of poets, many of whose names are familiar to scholars of the Renaissance, and, just as importantly, many who are obscure even among the informed. Honey divides the poems into four groups: Protest, Heritage, Love and Passion, and Nature, revealing the wide individual and collective interests of the writers. The majority of the women are included in more than one section. Honey claims that poetry was the preferred form of creative expression for the women writers of the 1920s, and from her text we see that these women made the widest possible use of the form. Scholars already familiar with some of these writers, and who are aware of their other writings, will observe that in specific instances, such as in the poetry of Angelina Weld Grimké and Georgia Douglas Johnson, the themes and motifs they employ here are also present in their plays. In choosing to include several selections from each writer, and for the better-known writers, to print examples of their lesser-known work, Honey's collection gives us an expanded appreciation of the intellectual concerns of black women in the 1920s. This has been especially important among those of us who have interests in black women's lives from the nineteenth to the middle of the twentieth century.

While nature is a common motif in much of this poetry, more interestingly, Honey identifies the ease with which some women, even those who were heterosexual, wrote about their love of female beauty. In this she suggests that the writers identified strongly with women as a whole and "affirmed that bond in their work," although not many were willing to explore erotic love for women in this public way. In the more recent work on the Harlem Renaissance we have come to realize that gay culture was part of the artistic circles of the time. This perhaps made it easier for the subject to appear, at least in a limited way, in women's poetry.

With limited opportunities to have their work appear in traditional (white) anthologies of American poetry, or to publish single volumes of their own, much of what Harlem Renaissance women wrote appeared in the leading black journals of their day, especially in *The Crisis* (the journal of the NAACP) and *Opportunity* (the journal of the Urban League). Since these were the most widely circulated and read of black media, these women, and the men whose work was published in the same places, were the most visible and widely read of the literary figures of their day. That these women appeared as often as they did in these journals indicates how well respected their work was by their peers, and how popular they must have been with readers.

The Introduction to *Shadowed Dreams* will be particularly useful for students and those less familiar with the writings of women of the period. There is much here to learn about the Renaissance in general. Honey sets the tone for a largely historical understanding of her writers, and her brief survey of the social events and important literary and artistic figures of the time will serve the uninitiated well. One striking similarity among the women poets is their membership in the educated black middle class of the time. As a result, many wrote what appears only as conventional, genteel verse. At the same time, Honey makes it clear that they were imaginative artists, and among them, there were a few who entertained ideological agendas and produced striking metaphors and poems of high aesthetic quality. Unquestionably, all believed in art, and this group of women took advantage of the temper of the times to participate in the cultural life of their group.

Black women poets of the Harlem Renaissance fully deserve the attention that Maureen Honey gives them in her book. Given the male domination of the New Negro movement, these were women who overcame many barriers in order to participate in the literary life of their time. With the high interest in all areas of women's lives at this time, this book is not only useful, it is vital to our understanding of a major area of Afro-American cultural history. And equally important, no longer will anyone be able to claim that the only major poets of the Renaissance were the men whose names have become the signatures for that movement over the past three decades. The women were there too!

Nellie Y. McKay
University of Wisconsin, Madison
December 1988

Acknowledgments

Three years ago, when I was researching a book on the 1920s, I discovered an astonishing number of poems by women in journals of the New Negro movement. Other scholars, I found, were revising contemporary assessments of the Harlem Renaissance in light of women's neglected accomplishments. Their work has paved the way for this anthology, in fact made it possible, and I wish to acknowledge my debt to them. Erlene Stetson, Ann Allen Shockley, and Deborah McDowell have all enriched our understanding of this period. I am especially grateful for the work of Gloria Hull who bravely brought to light the unpublished lesbian writings of Alice Dunbar-Nelson and Angelina Weld Grimké, ending a long critical silence on the role of lesbians in a key episode of Afro-American history. I thank her also for the kind, encouraging words with which she greeted a paper of mine on the political dimensions of women's nature poetry.

There are some contemporary poets who have also provided me with moral support for this project and whose work inspired me. Judy Grahn's enthusiasm led to my initial queries to publishers, June Jordan's artistry and friendship have helped me grow in ways essential to my scholarship, and Cheryl Clarke's interest in my work has reinforced my faith in this material. I give special thanks, too, to Joyletta Alice who provided me with motivation at points when I was the most doubtful of my ability to get these writers into print, insisting that women needed to have access to them and that I was on the right track.

I wish to express my gratitude to the University of Nebraska for its financial support of my research and to Roma Rector for her heroic transcription of these poems. I want to thank as well the copyright holders of these many poems for granting permission to reprint them, especially Chauncey E. Spencer, son of Anne Spencer, whose phone call was the high point of this project. I wish to extend also a big thank you to my editor Leslie Mitchner and to Barbara Christian for their feedback on the introduction. Their comments helped clarify my perspective and contributed to an improved final effort. Finally, I want to thank Nellie McKay for contributing her eloquent foreword to this volume. To have a scholar of her stature commenting on this material is a great honor.

Lincoln, Nebraska
December 1988

Shadowed Dreams

*"Oh Magalu, come! Take my hand and I will
read you poetry . . ."*
Helene Johnson, "Magalu" (1927)

Introduction

This is the first anthology to be devoted exclusively to women poets of the Harlem Renaissance. Since many critical works do not mention them at all, it is partly intended to balance the picture.[1] So many poems by women appeared during this time that we need a more representative sample than is now available to make judgments about the direction in which Black artists were moving. Furthermore, the era spanning the end of World War I to the Depression is distinguished in a number of important ways from those that preceded and followed it. The peculiar blend of romanticism, hedonism, anger, and faith in the capacity of art to effect change marks the twenties as a special time, one that has lessons for us today about the nature of racism and the Black artist's relationship to political change. For Black women, especially, this was a time of expansion, renewal, and promise, the collapse of which demands careful study if we are to understand the many challenges faced by Afro-American women writers yesterday and today.

Poetry was the preferred form of most Afro-American women writers during the 1920s. Well known in intellectual circles of their day and widely published, women poets achieved the respect of their peers and popularity with a middle-class audience. Scholars who lived through the Renaissance generally wrote favorably of them. Sterling Brown, for instance, compares Anne Spencer to Emily Dickinson and calls Georgia Douglas Johnson's poetry "skillful and fluent." James Weldon Johnson praises Gwendolyn Bennett for her "delicate, poignant" lyrics while calling attention to Jessie Fauset's "light and neat" touch.[2] Later critics, however, have tended to see women's verse as conventional and sentimental, out of step with the militant, rebellious race consciousness of the period.[3] Those who accord it some artistic value nevertheless agree that most women poets remained within the genteel school of "raceless" literature, having largely confined themselves to the realm of private experience and the natural world.[4] Known primarily for their lyrical, pastoral verse, women have been judged as imitating European traditions and contributing little that was useful to the creation of a Black aesthetic. Hampered by devotion to a theory of art not drawn from their own experience, so the consensus has been, whatever talent some of them exhibited was imprisoned by conformity to inappropriate models.

Any reappraisal of the women who participated in the Harlem Renaissance must begin with these twin misperceptions. In fact, much of their poetry exhibits the qualities of "New Negro" writing: identification with the race, a militant proud spirit, anger at racism, determination to fight oppression, rejection of white culture, and an attempt to reconstruct an invisible heritage. Even predominantly lyric poets produced verse concerned with protest and heritage. Anne Spencer, for instance, addressed lynching, female subordination, and racism while Georgia Douglas Johnson reflected often on prejudice and cultural imperialism. Indeed, fully half of the poetry by women published from 1918 through 1931 in those major journals of the Harlem Renaissance, *Opportunity* and *The Crisis*, dealt explicitly with race issues, and nearly as many women's poems were published as those by men.[5] Lynching, prejudice, stereotyping, white cultural imperialism, the assertion of rights, the strength of African ancestors and Black culture, and the beauty of their color, were all popular subjects during the decade for both men and women. Yet, as time went on, the image of women's poetry grew to be that of the pastoral or romantic lyric with only occasional reference to the vast number of race poems produced.[6]

Erlene Stetson, Gloria Hull, and Deborah McDowell are breaking new ground in criticism of women writers from this era by asserting that their art alludes, in a subversive way, to an oppressive social framework. McDowell has identified feminist, antiracist themes in Jessie Fauset's and Nella Larsen's work, for instance, two writers rather harshly judged as conventional and bourgeois. Gloria Hull connects the verse of Angelina Weld

Grimké, Alice Dunbar-Nelson, and Georgia Douglas Johnson to a larger framework of political writing and social activism. Finally, Erlene Stetson maintains that Black women's poetry is distinguished by subversive perception of the world and the use of subterfuge as a creative strategy. That their exploration takes place in a personal landscape, she asserts, should not detract from its radical implications.[7]

I subscribe to the critical models described above, and this anthology is intended to demonstrate that the full import of these poets' imaginative choices has been obscured for modern readers by their seemingly anachronistic style and subject matter. When placed in its historical context, however, their poetry comes alive, and its significance as an expression of the first modern Black female voice becomes clear. A new reading reveals that it is animated, not entirely by an imitative impulse, but rather by a defiant sensibility reflective of the rebellious women who wrote it. Because the total work of each writer was small (with the exception of Georgia Douglas Johnson), the pattern of metaphors and themes characteristic of women's writing is not evident when looking at individual poets.[8] The impulse behind their poetry, therefore, is unclear since the framework from which it emerged is invisible. Nevertheless, artistic choices were made repeatedly that give definition to individual poems seemingly divorced from a Black sensibility.

Although anthologizers are beginning to include women poets from this era, to my knowledge, this is the only one that arranges them thematically, an ordering that highlights their metaphorical continuities. Rather than representing a split consciousness, one that denies the Afro-American heritage of the writer, we can see how this poetry uses the landscape of nature and romantic love to affirm the humanity of women rendered invisible by the dominant culture. It forges a new consciousness hospitable to Black aspirations and culture. Black artists, particularly women, felt comfortable within these genres that provided opportunities to counter the destructive effects of racism and sexism.

Jessie Fauset is one of the writers who concentrated on the private world of romantic love in her poetry, yet she was a fervent supporter of Pan-Africanism and one of the prime movers of the

Harlem Renaissance. She stated, in fact (in 1922), that the issue of race was always with her: "I cannot if I will forget the fact of color in almost everything I do or say."[9] Anne Spencer, who excelled at lush descriptions of her garden, fought against racial discrimination in her small Virginia town and declared in a headnote to several of her poems: "I proudly love being a Negro woman."[10] Angelina Weld Grimké chose to write Imagistic nature poems and, at the same time, produced plays and short stories about lynching and sexual oppression. The seeming contrast between these women's personal struggles against racism and the non-racial quality of their poetry is a characteristic shared by many female poets of the time and can be properly understood only by reference to the political context in which the Harlem Renaissance occurred.

At the time of the Great Migration, Blacks found themselves under siege during an upsurge of terrorism both South and North. In the summer of 1919 alone, there were vicious attacks on the Black community in twenty-five cities and seventy people were lynched, with fourteen burned alive.[11] The Ku Klux Klan had been founded in 1915, D. W. Griffith had just filmed *Birth of a Nation*, and the blackface minstrel show was a standard act in vaudeville. With the breakdown of Progressivism after World War I, Blacks found little political support, and this, added to the reverses after Reconstruction, left them extremely vulnerable and isolated.[12]

The racial violence, political disenfranchisement, and racist propaganda of the post-Reconstruction period produced a movement among Blacks to educate white Progressives about the extent of reactionary violence against them and to upgrade the formal education of Blacks themselves. Bettina Aptheker has suggested that the focus on education, begun before Emancipation, grew out of a desire to fashion an informed leadership cadre that could spearhead moves toward legal, political, and economic power.[13] Communities were in desperate need of teachers, doctors, nurses, and lawyers they could trust. Furthermore, literacy and formal education, especially in the liberal arts, promised to demystify the defeated slaveholding class and dismantle the ideology of white supremacy, which held that Blacks were genetically incapable of intellectual activity or exercise of the "higher faculties," that is, reason and a cultured sensibility. Literacy posed a real threat to white supremacists because it not only opened avenues toward retrieving Afro-American history but also demolished the lie of Black intellectual inferiority with its corollary of white paternalism.[14]

The artists who came of age shortly before or during the Harlem Renaissance were raised by a generation newly emancipated, committed to education, and hungry for tangible accomplishments. They were made well aware of the value of good, sound schooling and its capacity to uplift the race, while sensing their importance as inheritors of the struggle for equality and opportunity. Nathan Huggins argues that individual achievement in the 1920s, particularly in the arts, which symbolized dramatic progress from slavery, connoted more than personal accomplishment. To the masses, it was a source of pride: "What may appear to us to be attitudes of bourgeois naiveté were very often highly race-conscious and aggressive."[15] The "Talented Tenth," as they were called by W. E. B. DuBois, could serve as living examples that Black inferiority was a myth serving to justify segregation and oppression. The Renaissance generation, therefore, conceived of itself as carrying on the struggle through attaining the highest possible level of literary accomplishment and surpassing the boundaries a racist society tried to impose. Writers saw no contradiction between social activism and the production of nonracial literature because the two were fused in their minds: artistic achievement moved the race upward.

Operating within the reactionary political climate after World War I, with Black people largely uneducated in a formal sense and unable to vote in the South, the vanguard of the Afro-American community had few options before it. Marcus Garvey's immensely appealing nationalistic call for Pan-African unity was aborted by Garvey's deportation in 1927 and seriously weakened by his imprisonment during the previous four years. In addition, the limitations of Booker T. Washington's entrepreneurial approach to rural poverty were being recognized. Meanwhile, racist parodying of Black folk culture was in full sway. These factors pushed artists closer to classical forms as they reached for tools that promised to transcend a bleak political situation.[16] The emotional need for a meaningful artistic tradition dovetailed with a narrowing of options in the 1920s to produce what Nathan Huggins correctly identifies as naive assumptions about the centrality of art to social change.[17] It is predictable, however, that in this largely middle-class group of artists only a few would be able to overcome their class- and race-biased education to draw on innovative Afro-American cadences for their work.

Huggins alludes to another impetus for the welding of politics and art typical of this generation, which was a belief in the reconstructive, transformative power of culture, a holdover from the Progressive movement. He suggests that most considered art a bridge between the races. They believed that artists were more likely to be free of prejudice,[18] because sensitivity and rationality could transcend political conflict. Intellect could overcome ignorance, break down alienation, and provide a bond between like-minded people of vastly different social castes. It was a position seemingly verified by the racial mixing that occurred in the salons of Harlem, Greenwich Village, and Paris and by the very real support for Black artists by whites like Carl Van Vechten, H. L. Mencken, Zona Gale, and others.[19]

The conventional verse for which Renaissance poets have been criticized was a logical outgrowth of this focus on literary achievement and the western humanistic tradition.[20] If mastering the poetic forms of a language forbidden their parents or grandparents was a political act, then viewing those forms as timeless and universal invested the act with even greater power. The sonnet, the ode, the elegy, and classical allusion when viewed platonically, as ideal forms, promised to provide a meeting ground, a common tongue, to which all might have access and by which all might be spiritually enlightened. There is no evidence that Harlem artists were conscious of the relationship between Western cultural domination (of which they had quite a sophisticated understanding) and their adoption of European literary forms. Even writers as innovative as Langston Hughes, who was personally close to pastoralist Anne Spencer, and Zora Neale Hurston, who when she tried her hand at poetry wrote lyric verse, failed to comment on the contradiction in form and intent that characterized most of their peers' work. Certainly, poets of the Renaissance did not consider the models they followed to be the province or reflection of the conqueror. Rather, these forms were conceived of as politically neutral vehicles through which Black culture could be made visible.[21]

The predominance of nature and love poetry is tangentially related to the appeal of Western literary forms, for, in looking to the classical tradition, poets were drawn to these subjects as expressions of a higher, more sublime plane than the problematic reality of daily life. Nineteenth-century Romantics were particularly compelling as models because they shared this generation's alienation from modern society, although not in a fully realized, articulated way. Byron, Wordsworth, Keats, Shelley, and Browning were important inspirational sources for Renaissance poets, because the Romantics saw art and truth as connected, a viewpoint that echoed their own sense that the ills of modern life stemmed from a coarsening of the human spirit due to acquisitive, aggressive domination by a white ruling class.[22] Nature offered an Edenesque alternative to the corrupted, artificial environment created by "progress."

In this way, Harlem intellectuals shared in the revulsion of many contemporary white artists toward what they believed to be a world run by morally bankrupt leaders.[23] Similarly, they looked to the body and sensuality for vitality as did writers of the 1920s who, influenced by Freud, rebelled against Victorian prudery.[24] While Afro-Americans were skeptical of the phenomenon that came to be known as "primitivism," they, too, were drawn to a vision of releasing creative energy through plumbing one's natural drives, particularly the erotic.[25] When Virginia Houston writes about "the ecstacy / Of soft lips covering mine, / Dragging my soul through my mouth," or Kathleen Tankersley Young calls her lover's body "a dark wine" that will "let [her] body and soul go free," they are expressing the notion that erotic impulses are connected to liberation of the self, a commonly held idea in the 1920s.[26]

As Afro-Americans, women poets were sensitive to the political and artistic currents affecting Black men of their day, but as women, they drew special meaning from them. Alienated by a technological urban world that excluded Blacks and operated for self-interest rather than social justice, women also saw the cityscape as manmade. Although Harlem is celebrated in their poetry, the urban environment is primarily represented as alien and intrusive. Bessie Mayle's "Skylines" describes the oppressive effect of city life on her writing when she complains that skyscrapers are "huge arms" hampering her movement, "mountains" that encircle her "valley." "Huge things are jealous things," she tells us, locking her out of a world that nourishes the self. Similarly, Marjorie Marshall vows to leave the city in "Nostalgia" because "the rigid cry / Of steel on stone" has drowned out her own songs and drained her of creative energy.

Nature, in contrast, is presented as nurturing, life-giving, a haven from strife. It is also personified as female. Effie Lee Newsome refers to dew as "Night's pregnant tears" in "Morning Light (The Dew-Drier)," Mae Cowdery rests on "the sable breast / Of earth" in "Longings," and Helene Johnson leans against "a strong tree's bosom" in "Fulfillment."

Sharing the pastoral vision of male poets like Countée Cullen and Claude McKay, women had added reason to locate the self in natural settings. Nature provided an objective correlative through which they could articulate their gender oppression as well as that of race, for nature, like them, had been objectified, invaded, and used by men seeking power and wealth.[27] At times, nature is brought to life as a woman, and the poet evokes for her our sympathy or admiration. The river in Ethel Caution's poem of the same name, for instance, is described as "a decrepit old woman / Shivering in her sombre shawl of fog" while the moon is a woman searching for her children in Esther Popel's "Theft." The connection between male domination, white supremacy, and the destruction of nature is evident in Anne Spencer's "White Things." She begins with a statement that most things on this earth are "colorful" but that the single race without color is the one that dominates: "Most things are colorful things—the sky, earth, and sea. / Black men are most men; but the white are free!" In a sophisticated analysis of power lust, Spencer likens the colonization process to a draining of nature's vitality when she says that white men "blanched with their wand of power" all with which they came in contact:

> Finding earth-plains fair plains, save greenly grassed,
> They strewed white feathers of cowardice, as they passed;
>   The golden stars with lances fine,
>   The hills all red and darkened pine,
> They blanched with their wand of power;
> And turned the red in a ruby rose
> To a poor white poppy-flower.

Abruptly, Spencer shifts her focus to terrorism against Blacks in the second stanza, ending with a chilling image of one member of a lynch mob laughingly swinging a skull "in the face of God," enjoining his deity to turn the world white:

> They pyred a race of black, black men,
> And burned them to ashes white; then,
> Laughing, a young one claimed a skull,
> For the skull of a black is white, not dull,
>   But a glistening awful thing
>   Made, it seems, for this ghoul to swing
> In the face of God with all his might,
> And swear by the hell that sired him:
>   'Man-maker, make white!'

While the poem mentions neither Native Americans nor women, it concerns both. Spencer wrote these lines after reading about a woman, pregnant at the time, tortured by a lynch mob in 1918. She had been trying to protect her husband, who had killed his employer, a farmer known for his vicious treatment of Black laborers.[28] The reference to colonization of Native Americans can be found in the first stanza where the arrival of Europeans is described in line four: "They stole from out a silvered world— somewhere." The poet then metaphorically places the original inhabitants of these "earth-plains" in the landscape by referring to "hills all red" which the colonizer paradoxically turned white with his bloody attack. The metaphor is extended in lines ten and eleven where, we are told, whites "turned the blood in a ruby rose / To a poor white poppy-flower." Spencer identified strongly with Native Americans (her father was half Seminole and she frequently wore her long, straight hair in braids).[29] Here, she makes a connection between their defeat and terrorism against Afro-Americans, linking both to the mad desire of a minority race to destroy everything unlike itself.

When Spencer first submitted this poem for publication, she was told by the editors that they would delete a stanza referring to "white men" which appeared in the original version because, as a newly emerging Afro-American writer (this was one of her first poems to appear in print), she could not afford to alienate white publishers.[30] This incident sheds light on the veiled references to race and gender oppression that appear in women's poetry of the Harlem Renaissance. Black artists were vulnerable in a political situation where Afro-Americans were still struggling to form a power base. Not only could women identify with a natural landscape that men dominated and violated, but the identification afforded them metaphors for describing their oppression in ways subversive of white male power yet indirect enough not to offend that very group.

Whiteness, for instance, is a malevolent force in their poetry, associated with invisibility, suffocation, and death. The poem "Chalk-Dust" by Lillian Byrnes illustrates this characteristic feature well. It concerns the desire of a teacher to escape her classroom and "to roll in wet, green grass, / To plunge headfirst into youth, and music, and laughter." Chalk-dust permeates the air, her hair, and clothing, symbolizing the dry, lifeless facts written on her blackboard: "It has the relentless persistence of the long dead. / It gets between me and the rays of the sun / . . . It will strangle me slowly, quietly; / And sift over my body when I, like it, / Am so dead as to be merely useful." The world of book knowledge is white and suffocating while colorful nature releases a life-giving, joyous sensuality. Similarly, the white light of the moon is portrayed as a demon that will steal the soul of a mother's baby in African writer Aqua Laluah's poem "Lullaby": "Close your sleepy eyes, or the pale moonlight will steal you, / Else in the mystic silence, the moon will turn you white. / Then you won't see the sunshine, nor smell the open roses, / Nor love your Mammy anymore, whose skin is dark as night. / . . . Wherever moonlight stretches her arms across the heavens, / You will follow, . . . till you become instead, / A shade in human draperies." Here, Laluah creates an allegory for the process by which Black people become separated from their roots through using the moon as a symbol of white culture. If you gaze too long at images of whiteness, the mother warns her child, you will reject your racial heritage and conform to alien standards, thereby becoming a shadow self.

A more complicated use is made of white metaphors in Esther Popel's "Theft." The moon is described as an old woman looking in vain for her children, afraid of and taunted by the elements as she hurries home. She creeps along, huddled in an old black cape, and tries to escape the wind who pelts her with snowballs, "filling her old eyes with the flakes of them." Suddenly she falls and is buried by the snow while jewels fall from her bag onto earth whereupon they are seized by tall trees, which then sparkle with their "glittering plunder." The trees are uncharacteristically ominous in this poem, but the usage of moon and snow are typical. The snow blinds this old woman, trips and envelops her; it causes her to lose a small treasure carefully guarded. Finally, its companion, the wind, laughs at her piteous moans and turns her own children against her who, though found, prove to be enemies. Negative white elements are present in a double sense here: the desperate mother is defeated by them, and she is herself white, or rather yellow, the color of old white paint. Popel's central figure is ambiguous in that she evokes pity, modifying the image of the moon as dangerous. At the same time, she represents weakness, debility, and devastating loss.

Allusions to white domination and danger abound, yet the predominant message encourages resistance and survival. Alice Dunbar-Nelson's reflections on a snow-covered autumn tree, for instance, focus on its resilience under a heavy burden: "Today I saw a thing of arresting poignant beauty: / A strong young tree, brave in its Autumn finery / . . . Bending beneath a weight of early snow, / Which . . . spread a heavy white chilly afghan / Over its crested leaves. / Yet they thrust through, defiant, glowing, / Claiming the right to live another fortnight." While Dunbar-Nelson's ostensible subject is aging, the notion of defying a deathly white power is at the core of the poem.

Angelina Weld Grimké's piece, "Tenebris," echoes this subtle assertion of self against white control:

> There is a tree by day
> That at night
> Has a shadow,
> A hand huge and black,
> With fingers long and black.
>   All through the dark,
> Against the white man's house,
>   In the little wind,
> The black hand plucks and plucks
>   At the bricks.
> The bricks are the color of blood and very small.
>   Is it a black hand,
>   Or is it a shadow?

By likening the branches of a tree to a hand "huge and black," whose shadow rests against "the white man's house," Grimké invites us to find in her image a statement about the relationship of Blacks to white society. One reading of the poem is that it sees Black struggle as a subterranean, persistent chipping away at white structures. The black hand "plucks and plucks" at the bricks, which are "the color of blood and very small," at night, when the occupant is sleeping, falsely secure that the image on his house is the shadow of a harmless tree. Yet the last line asks: "Is it a black hand, or is it a shadow?" and we are left sensing that the white man's house is in danger. The portrait of a house built with blood-colored bricks evokes memories of the big house on a plantation maintained by the blood and sweat of slave labor. It is also haunted by the ghosts of people whose anguish and anger are growing shadows on the white man's power, gathering force while he basks in his privilege.

Images of entrapment, masking, and burial appear regularly in these poems, at times explicitly in conjunction with references to men. Blanche Taylor Dickinson, for instance, protests being surrounded by walls that limit her existence to a room and keep her from wandering freely through life. The speaker longs for the strength of Samson so she can break her bondage to "this conscious world with guarded men" but fears that she has internalized their rules to a point where freedom would have no meaning. [31] Another poem of Dickinson's that implies women are constrained by a male force is "To an Icicle," which warns against having a false sense of security in a world governed by those who are physically stronger: "Chilled into a serenity / As rigid as your pose / You linger trustingly, / But a gutter waits for you. / Your elegance does not secure / You favors with the sun. / He is not one to pity fragileness. / He thinks all cheeks should burn / And feel how tears can run." The allusion to the home as imprisoning in Dickinson's "Four Walls" is made as well in Georgia Douglas Johnson's "Wishes," where the speaker complains: "I'm tired of pacing the petty round of the ring of the thing I know— / I want to stand on the daylight's edge and see where the sunsets go." The image of a wedding ring is evoked to demonstrate the confinement of marriage with its "petty" tasks and movement toward nowhere while the world lies waiting for exploration. In like fashion, Effie Lee Newsome chides men for denying women their freedom in "The Bird in the Cage:" "I am not better than my brother over the way, / Only he has a bird in the cage and I have not."

Restlessness pervades poetry of the decade along with laments about the inability to move or travel very far away from home. Horizons beckon, roads appear, yet the speaker is rooted to one spot. Some critics have suggested that these poets relied on imagination, dream, and rumination to extricate them from a painful reality. Ronald Primeau, for example, identifies this impulse as central to Georgia Douglas Johnson's work. He believes she exalts creativity because it can fashion a world that does not exist, one where it is possible to imagine freedom and beauty even when they cannot be realized. [32] This theme can be found in the writing of Angelina Weld Grimké, too, as her speakers sit at the edge of an ocean and dream of sailing to unknown places, or gaze out a window at twilight, reflecting on the emerging stars. As Gloria Hull notes, Grimké's personae are often submerged, diminished;[33] yet, their mind's eye is focused on intense images that hint at infinite spaces. Anne Spencer's verse is also characterized by marked contrast between the sordidness of the material plane and the speaker's imaginary world of love and natural beauty.[34] Lyric poetry, then, became a vehicle for movement, since it transported both poet and reader to a place where women could feel safe, unbound, and powerful.

The use of trees in these poems is common, for trees are stationary, as women are immobilized by confining roles. Symbolic of paralysis, they can nevertheless be viewed positively. In Grimké's "The Black Finger," a tree's silhouette is highlighted by sunset: "I have just seen a most beautiful thing: / Slim and still, / Against a gold, gold sky, / A straight, black cypress / Sensitive / Exquisite / A black finger / Pointing upwards." Leading the eye toward a vast, open space where the soul can soar, the tree in this poem can, in some sense, stand for the miraculous survival of Black aspiration as the poet ends by asking: "Why, beautiful still finger, are you black? / And why are you pointing upwards?" Helene Johnson employs the same metaphor in "Trees at Night" where she draws an image of vibrant wonder crystallized by the interplay of light and shadow on a moonlit night: "Slim sentinels / Stretching lacy arms / About a slumbrous moon; / Black quivering / Silhouettes, / Tremulous, / . . . And printed 'gainst the sky— / The trembling beauty / Of an urgent pine." It is the silhouette of the tree that attracts the poet's eye, the intricate pattern of branches against a sky, the stillness of a solid trunk anchored by sure roots and pushing against the force of gravity. The trunk's rich brownness is starkly highlighted in silhouette, devoid of obscuring foliage and beautiful in its hardy survival of harsh conditions. The poetic tree transcends its condition of immobility to stand for quiet endurance, pride, dignity, and aspiration. Like women, it has a delicate beauty under the toughness that enables it to survive.

An even more pronounced poetic strategy allowing for metamorphosis is the personification of night as a woman whose powers are both protective and liberating. While night in its color offers an obvious parallel as a source of self-imagery, it is conventionally feared as a time of danger, a space inhabited by frightening supernatural beings. Night symbolizes the unknown, the absence of reason and control, the antithesis of conscious awareness. These are also properties assigned to Black people and to women. Having felt the sting of "otherness," poets identified with a dark power, feared and maligned. In rescuing night from negative fantasies and imbuing it with creative force, the writer could heal the stigma of distorted perceptions.

"What do I care for morning," asks Helene Johnson, "For the glare of the rising sun . . . ? / . . . Give me the beauty of evening, / The cool consummation of night."[35] The preference for nighttime over day expressed in Johnson's poem is marked in women's poetry and served a variety of functions. One of these was to assert the primacy of Blackness in a world that favored white things. Quieter, calmer, less dramatic than the day, night was, nevertheless, an essential force in life, the contemplation of which brought serenity to a restless, discontented spirit. Gwendolyn Bennett's Imagist portrait, "Street Lamps in Early Spring," is typical in its elegiac tone:

> Night wears a garment
> All velvet soft, all violet blue . . .
> And over her face she draws a veil
> As shimmering fine as floating dew . . .
> And here and there
> In the black of her hair
> The subtle hands of Night
> Move slowly with their gem-starred light.

Overlooked by the insensitive, the beauty of Blackness and femaleness is here brought from the background to center stage and admired for its steady, subtle force.

Bennett's poem captures another aspect of night's usefulness as an image for Black women. Night is said to draw over her face a veil "shimmering fine as floating dew." Cast as a goddess whose features are hidden, night stands for the masked self, obscured by the fears and projected fantasies of gazers with the power to define. Although night is veiled in mystery, she escapes the distorted, negative images of those who fail to see her clearly. Self-assured, she parades through poetry of the twenties with regal grace. The donning of a mask for self-protection, then, does not forever submerge the vital, beautiful person underneath, who possesses powers unrecognized by the world.

Not only a vibrant woman of great spirit who rules her domain wisely, night offers respite from the daily struggle to survive, for in a dark world, Blackness cannot be used as a marker of difference. Since there is no need to dissemble, the poet can come alive in her presence: "Last night I danced on the rim of the moon, / Delirious and gay, / Quite different from the mood / I wear about by day. / . . . And oh! my feet flew madly! / My body whirled and swayed! / My soul danced in its ecstasy, / Untrammeled, unafraid!" (Ethel M. Caution). "Within the shadow of the moon you danced / . . . Your dark flame-beauty challenging a glance; / You flung a sob-caught laugh and leaped afar / Into the arms of night, with upturned face / That mocked the waning beauty of the moon" (Marjorie Marshall). "To dance— / In the light of the moon, / A platinum moon, / Poised like a slender dagger / On the velvet darkness of night" (Mae V. Cowdery).[36] The images of movement here contrast sharply with the references to deathlike stillness that appear elsewhere, and the poets celebrate the activation of their creative energy. While women looked to natural settings in general for space in which to savor the freedom from confining roles, night was sought most frequently, as it was a time when the objectifying eye was closed in sleep and the freedom to be at one with the soul could be safely enjoyed.

It is also to night that the poet turns for solace and restoration. In "Want," Mae Cowdery makes use of this convention when she soothes herself through communing with the stars and moon: "I want to take down with my hands / The silver stars / That grow in heaven's dark blue meadows / And bury my face in them. / I want to wrap all around me / The silver shedding of the moon / To keep me warm." The reference to night as comforter transforms it from a setting of terror, a time when Black people were tormented by white vigilantes, into one of peace. Poems centered on lynching victims, for instance, commonly close on a note of relief wherein night mercifully descends to remove a man's soul from his tortured body. The images of softness linked to night indicate its association with a mother's comforting embrace. Consoler of the bruised and even broken spirit, guardian of the soul at rest, night serves as a metaphor for the restorative powers within to which the poet can turn when feelings of despair overwhelm her. Just as the death of each day is followed by a healing period of quiet repose, so, too, does the battered spirit find sustenance in womblike suspension of interaction with the outside world.

The impulse to protect oneself from a hurtful reality is not an admission of defeat, but, rather, an acknowledgment that the forces arrayed against a Black woman's dignity and development of her powers are formidable. Anne Spencer's poem, "Letter to My Sister," develops this idea and provides insight into the motif of retreat found in poetry about night. Though the gods she mentions are not identified as male, it is made clear that women battle a common enemy and share a kind of bondage that sets them apart from men. "It is dangerous for a woman to defy the gods," she begins, "To taunt them with the tongue's thin tip / . . . Or draw a line daring them to cross." The speaker adds, however, that appeasement will not protect women from harm: "Oh, but worse still if you mince timidly— / Dodge this way or that, or kneel or pray." Instead, she recommends deftly removing one's treasured secrets from view and revealing them only in strict privacy: "Lock your heart, then quietly, / And, lest they peer within, / Light no lamp when dark comes down / Raise no shade for sun." Although the day's piercing light destroys, it can be thwarted by guarding the innermost recesses of the self.

Michael Cooke has identified self-veiling as a major stage in the development of Afro-American literature, one that occurred in the early part of his century and extended through the 1920s.[37] His terminology aptly describes women's nature poetry—indirect, coded, wrung free of overt anger. Yet it would be a mistake to view this verse as divorced from issues of race, gender, or oppression. The theme of regeneration through retreat and disguise echoes the actual practice of poets searching for a way to make themselves heard without facing annihilation. It also suggests avoidance of more frontal assaults on an overwhelmingly power-ful enemy. This would have been a realistic strategy in the twen-ties, particularly for women whose formative years occurred in the terrible repression that followed Reconstruction.

Another Spencer poem, "Lady, Lady," brings to the surface the three major themes of women's poetry (equation of Blackness and femaleness with strength, resistance to white male oppres-sion, survival of the core self) and illustrates how they are inter-twined with nature metaphors. Typical of much Renaissance poetry, it studies a member of the working class, a launderer, made invisible by racism and classism. The washerwoman bears the stamp of her oppressor. Her face has been chiseled by pain from carrying "the yoke of men"; her hands are twisted "like crumpled roots" by the labor she does for white people, symboliz-ing the stunting of her growth and crippling of her true posture. They are also "bleached poor white," a sign of her consignment to a draining, exploited existence controlled by whites. Despite the harsh life she has led, however, there remains a sacred invio-lable place within her where a spirit burns brightly, "altared there in its darksome place," host to a transcendent guiding force.

Women's search for roots and identity led inward, moved backward to an imaginary Eden where sensitivity could survive and even flourish. For writers who largely could not travel to Eu-rope or Africa, the concept of a hidden self, rich with wisdom, offered an attractive substitute for an unknown, removed history. Moreover, it was accessible and consistent with the Romantic no-tion that truth lies within, uncorrupted by one's external circum-stances.[38] Bernard Bell suggests, in fact, that the Romantic, pas-toral aspect of literature during the Harlem Renaissance might be best understood as ancestralism, arising from a desire to reconcile the urban present with a rural past: "Out of a sense of loss, a feeling that the times were out of joint and the soul was under siege, . . . a romantic longing for a freer, more innocent time and place was born: . . . where the rhythms of life were closely linked to nature and one's essential humanity was unquestioned . . . that fostered a feeling of harmony . . . with one's ancestors [and] one's self."[39] It is possible, then, to detect an affirmation of the poet's own gen-der and race in pastoral lyrics, for retreat to the preindustrial past or the self within furnished ties to a heritage dimly glimpsed and a locale more hospitable to the emergence of female power.

Women's pastoral verse is indirect and masked, but their love poetry is an attempt to speak in a straightforward and authentic manner. It too grows out of a preoccupation with the Romantics in that passionate attachments were thought to elevate one's spirit above the plane of normal existence to a sublime state of intensified experience. Here the uncorrupted soul could fully express the self. Even heartache was viewed as purifying, because it proved that the poet had dared to share a real part of herself with someone; it was evidence of an unmasked encounter.

Seemingly unconnected to social issues, this poetry appears, at first glance, to be an anomalous feature of a literary movement to break free of stereotypes and record the Afro-American experience. Yet it reverberates with emotions that implicitly challenged the dehumanizing caricatures of Black people found in American culture. For instance, one of the many misconceptions held by white people at the time was that Blacks were a happy race, perpetually childlike in their ability to laugh at woe and shrug off cares. Such an image served important psychological functions for whites, among them relief from guilt, allaying fears about rebellion, and escape from a sober model of propriety.[40] A laughing Black face put whites at ease and seemingly offered a world where troubles could be left behind. New Negro writers addressed this issue by making public their rage at having to hide so much of themselves in order to fulfill white fantasies. When read in this context, the love poetry takes on added significance, for in it, the poet reveals her pain, her human capacity to be vulnerable and suffer deep disappointment. She possesses the gift of laughter, but it is clear that sadness has shaped her as much as joy, that suffering is a part of her life.

The heartbreak over unrequited love that runs through this poetry also asserts that the personal realm of the poet need not be uplifting in order to be a proper subject for public verse. All feelings are worthy of poetic expression. This claiming of the despondent self represented an important departure from nineteenth-century Afro-American poetry which followed that era's conception of art as something that should inspire and instruct. It was, therefore, incumbent on the poet to be optimistic and end poems on a forward-looking note.[41] Insisting on the full range of human emotions for their province, poets of the twenties expanded the boundaries of acceptable subjects to include despair and woeful yearning after something lost.

The right, indeed the necessity, to recognize anguish as a consequence of being fully alive is a theme often struck in this poetry of the heart. Refusing to take the safer, yet diminished, path of a life without dreams or large emotional risks, the poet proclaims that her suffering produces growth. Emotional transport, whether toward joy or sorrow, is heralded as a life force that brings the speaker into contact with her humanity and the world around her. It is both her route to self-actualization, as she is willing to encounter life directly, and her announcement that she is multidimensional, a woman of sensitivity and passion.

In evaluating the significance of Renaissance love poetry, it is important to keep in mind that a fundamental tenet of white supremacy was that Afro-Americans were not capable of fine, romantic feelings. Lindsay Patterson is careful to point this out in his anthology of love poetry by Black writers from Angelina Weld Grimké to Sonia Sanchez, stating that denigration of bonding among slaves was one of the primary forms of control exerted by slaveholders over their property. He believes it is affirming, therefore, to make visible an Afro-American tradition of love poetry and to see it as a form of resistance.[42] One way to dehumanize an oppressed group, of course, is to strip it of the capacity to form meaningful attachments, and Black writers of the twenties were well acquainted with caricatures that implied they were unromantic people.

Furthermore, the frankly erotic dimension of women's poetry negated desexed images of the plantation mammy, immensely popular at the time with a white audience. The mammy was a safe figure, particularly for the white female imagination, because she wanted only to take care of her employer (mystifying the exploitative relationship between them) and posed no sexual competition.[43] Divorced from sexuality, the mammy, like her Uncle Tom counterpart, was simplified for her role as caretaker. To bring their bodies into public view under their own terms was to state that Black women were sentient, complex beings deserving of sexual pleasure, a statement also being made by jazz and blues singers of the 1920s, who were expanding the boundaries of female sexual expression as well as Afro-American music.

On the other hand, women as mothers were glorified by male artists of the Harlem Renaissance. The frontispiece to Alain Locke's *The New Negro*, for example, is a portrait of a young woman cradling a baby, entitled "The Brown Madonna."[44] Indeed, one of the primary metaphors of the New Negro movement was that of the young mother leading the race to a brighter day.[45] As a representation of rebirth, such an image was irresistible and women, too, made use of it but more ambivalently. Often, for instance, birth is distanced by embedding it in a natural landscape described as pregnant or maternal. Though mothers and babies appear in their verse, child-rearing or nurturing roles are not favored topics. In turning so often in poems to moments of erotic passion, women suggested that they valued most highly those relationships they could enter as autonomous persons and from which they could fashion adventurous lives. Many of these poets were, in fact, single or childless. Some were lesbians, and those who were married often refused to assume domestic burdens and were social activists as well as writers.[46] These were women in flight from Victorianism and their verse claims sexual independence. The refusal of Harlem poets to hide female passion was resistance to being defined as selfless nurturers or as anyone's property. Romantic passion existed outside the boundaries of marriage and Victorian conceptions of womanhood as well as beyond racist stereotypes of the mammy or the "African primitive."

What Lillian Faderman has described as "passionate friendships" between women had been forged in life and described in literature throughout the Victorian period, but they were depicted in sentimental terms.[47] The eroticism found in verse of the 1920s not only made visible the hunger of Black women for unrestricted, self-defining experience, but also brought to the surface feelings for women that had been couched previously in platonic language. After World War I, women's verse began to explore the forbidden territory of explicit sexual attraction. Only two female writers from this era have been identified as feeling passionate attraction to other women: Alice Dunbar-Nelson and Angelina Weld Grimké. Gloria Hull brought to light both Dunbar-Nelson's diary entries concerning her attachments to women and Grimké's overtly lesbian unpublished poetry.[48] There are others, however, who went beyond the veiled lesbianism of Grimké's published work and Dunbar-Nelson's poetic silence on the subject.

Gladys May Casely Hayford's "Rainy Season Love Song," for instance, is addressed to a woman referred to as "my love" in the first stanza. The persona of the poem describes making love to this figure in a rainstorm that shares the speaker's desire. Rain kisses her "everywhere," flows between her breasts, while lightning and thunder move inside her body. The speaker kisses her beloved's "dusky throat," feels electricity wherever she touches, and, finally, lies in her lover's arms. While not as overtly sexual, Hayford's "The Serving Girl" creates a similarly erotic milieu as the speaker describes an encounter with the woman of the title, who brings fish "peppered, and golden fried for me" along with palm wine "that carelessly slips / From the sleeping palm tree's honeyed lips." The poem then ends with a provocative question: "But who can guess, or even surmise / The countless things she served with her eyes?" Mae V. Cowdery wrote love poems to women also. In her collection *We Lift Our Voices*, she included "Insatiate," which concerns the speaker's intense jealousy over her female lover, while three other published pieces suggest a lesbian relationship. In one, the poet says the onset of dusk is "Like you / Letting down your / Purple-shadowed hair / To hide the rose and gold / Of your loveliness." "Farewell" is subtler but implies the loss of a female lover when the speaker refers to "the rumpled softness" of her lost love's hair and "the lush sweetness" of her lips, "like dew / On new-opened moonflowers." Finally, in "Poem . . . for a Lover," the speaker's object of longing is said to possess "gay little songs" and "lips . . . redder / Than bitter-sweet berries."

The appearance of such poetry was made possible, in part, by the support of Alain Locke and Countée Cullen who were themselves gay and committed to frank expression of sensuality in verse.[49] An important anthology of the period was Cullen's *Caroling Dusk*, which included the most comprehensive array of women poets assembled to that date and featured Hayford's two most suggestive, woman-centered pieces.[50] Cullen's own verse, of course, shared many of the features found in women's writing, including a reverence for nineteenth-century Romantics, most notably Keats, and a tendency to focus on love. His sensibility was in tune with theirs, and he has been subjected to similarly harsh contemporary criticism.[51] Alain Locke's intellectual leanings were, perhaps, even more instrumental in creating a tolerant atmosphere for lesbian writing. While by no means a friend to women artists (he often pointedly neglected them), his philosophical leadership in the New Negro movement fostered acceptance of the kind of writing they were doing.[52] An openness toward lesbianism, specifically, is suggested in his foreword to Georgia Douglas Johnson's collection *An Autumn Love Cycle*, where he praises her for joining that group of women "rediscovering the Sapphic cult of love."[53] He also thought highly of Mae Cowdery.[54]

Renewed attention to the Harlem Renaissance is revealing, in fact, that gay and lesbian culture was very much a part of Harlem artistic circles. Lesbian singers Bessie Smith, Ma Rainey, and Gladys Bentley, for instance, were star performers during the twenties and their sexual preferences were known to those who frequented jazz clubs.[55] In addition, the primary organizers of Harlem social life, A'Lelia Walker and Carl Van Vechten, routinely sought the company of lesbians and gay men and invited them to their parties.[56] The intellectual and social atmosphere in which Renaissance writers worked, therefore, at least did not condemn lesbianism.

It is, perhaps, this tolerance that allowed women to explore their love for other women less self-consciously than they had in the past. Even poets who were evidently heterosexual, such as Anne Spencer, Gwendolyn Bennett, and Georgia Douglas Johnson, wrote freely about loving women, suggesting that these writers identified strongly with women as a whole and affirmed that bond in their work. It took courage to write about woman-love in a period when psychologists were developing modes of illness for lesbians.[57] Although only a handful of poems dating from this era overtly expressed erotic attraction for women, their existence marks the earliest body of literature to deal with this subject by Black women. It would take another forty years for such poetic voices to be heard again.

The characteristics and significance of women's poetry during the Harlem Renaissance can, perhaps, best be understood by closely examining three representative figures. Anne Spencer is the first of these, arguably the most accomplished of the women poets. Typical of most women's low output, she published less than thirty poems between 1920 and 1931, in spite of enthusiastic responses from leading figures of the period such as James Weldon Johnson. In addition, Spencer's poetry conforms to contemporary notions about women. It is pastoral, convoluted, and heavily influenced by the classical training she received at the seminary in Lynchburg, Virginia, where she spent her teenage years. Her favorite poet was Robert Browning. It is the lyric poetry of Spencer, Grimké, and Dunbar-Nelson that was most likely to be included in later anthologies of Afro-American verse, and, thus, their poems have had to bear the weight of all those excluded.

It is instructive to look at Anne Spencer's life and publishing history, for they explode the mythology that has developed around writers conceived of as bourgeois, apolitical artists who failed to produce innovative work.[58] While Spencer and her husband led a comfortable life in rural Virginia, her roots were in poverty. Spencer's parents were former slaves who left their plantation birthplace to establish independent lives. Determined not to work for a white man, her father, Joel, opened a saloon in Martinsville, Virginia, where he frequently had Anne perform for his customers as she was a bright, attractive child. Sarah, Anne's mother, left her husband when he refused to stop taking his daughter to the bar and supported them both with difficulty, becoming a cook in a West Virginia mining town. Unable to look after her child while at work, Anne's mother placed her with the family of a Black barber in nearby Bramwell.[59]

Spencer's childhood, therefore, was marked by disruption and financial hardship. Although she was well cared for, she had no formal education until age eleven, when Sarah sent her to Virginia Seminary, apparently to get her away from the white men of

Bramwell before she hit adolescence.[60] So sensitive was Spencer about her parents' early adult lives that she refused to provide her biographer with surnames.[61] She acquired a keen sense of how it felt to live on the periphery of American society, identifying at an early age with outcasts and rebels. She refused to be "a lady," resisting rules at the seminary, wearing pants as an adult, and protesting the exclusion of Blacks from the library in Lynchburg, among other things. In short, Anne Spencer, the woman, was unconventional, politically active, and passionate in her opposition to injustice.

These qualities are reflected in her writing, although not in the pieces for which she is best known. Two unpublished poems, for instance, written during the Renaissance era, reveal her commitment to social justice and the far-reaching nature of her political vision. "The Sévignés" was prompted by an article Spencer read in a 1930 issue of *National Geographic* describing a new monument that had just been erected of an "old-time darkey" in Natchitoches, Louisiana, to commemorate Harriet Beecher Stowe's *Uncle Tom's Cabin.* Spencer was offended by the servility of the statue and the slaveholding history it uncritically recalled. Her poem parallels the racism of twentieth-century America with the callousness of the seventeenth-century aristocrat Marquise de Sévigné, whose letters revealed gross insensitivity to sufferings of the poor. The poem not only connects a corrupt aristocracy with a supposed democracy but also points out the hypocrisy of French immigrants who left Europe to escape oppression and then enslaved people themselves: "No penance, callous beyond belief, / For these women who had so lately fled from the slavery of Europe to the great wilds of America."[62] Spencer's sensitivity to the general issue of colonization is evident here, in her poem "White Things," and in another unpublished piece about the struggle for freedom in Ireland. The last focuses on Terence MacSwiney, who died in 1922 after a seventy-four-day hunger strike protesting English rule. The poem's subject is the awakening of a rebel whose childhood was spent in carefree ignorance of the system that oppressed him. Once aware that the rich are housed in stone and the poor in hovels, he dedicates his life to overturning the state.[63]

The nature poetry, at which Spencer excelled, frequently was animated by subtle references to racism or sexism. J. Lee Greene, for example, interprets "Grapes: Still-Life" as an allegorical portrait of people of color and tells us that "Creed," a poem with no reference to race, was inspired by the poet's visit to Harpers Ferry, scene of the slave revolt led by John Brown.[64] More pointedly aimed at power relations, "Before the Feast at Shushan" concerns a rebellious Persian queen, chronicled in the Old Testament, who tries to establish an egalitarian relationship with her husband, the speaker of the poem. Yet the feminist message is masked by the king's archaic language and his use of metaphor to articulate chauvinist ideas. Significantly, the metaphors are drawn from flora and fauna: King Ahasuerus compares kissing Queen Vashti to crushing a grape and declares his right to rape her when he boasts "And I am hard to force the petals wide." Indeed, the setting for Ahasuerus's monologue about the resisting Vashti's charms is a garden which, he says, "enspells the brain." Pastoral beauty is a backdrop against which the ugliness of prejudice, hatred, and domination is effectively juxtaposed. Dividing her time between cultivating a splendid garden in Lynchburg and intensely discussing politics with out-of-town guests, Spencer blended her two passions in lyrics whose import may not be clear to those unaware of their context.

When she wrote the poem about Terence MacSwiney, Spencer sent it to the *Manchester Guardian*, hoping it would be published in England. It was, not surprisingly, rejected, and the incident explains the direction women poets had to take during the Renaissance. Blunt and politically astute, Spencer reported in her last years that she was discouraged from writing racial protest poems by editors, critics, and friends and that the prose she wrote, but never published, was "topical and controversial,"[65] a writing pattern shared by Georgia Douglas Johnson, Alice Dunbar-Nelson, and Angelina Weld Grimké.[66] We can only speculate on the degree to which those writers, too, were steered away from political poetry, but Spencer's experience hints at the difficulties they all had in breaking out of the formats considered acceptable for women's verse.

Helene Johnson is, in many ways, Anne Spencer's opposite.

She was one of the period's youngest writers, whereas Spencer did not publish until she was nearly forty. Although Spencer's rural home in Lynchburg was a frequent stopping-place for writers, musicians, and NAACP organizers, she never set foot in New York, while Johnson planted herself squarely in Harlem. Finally, Johnson's best poetry is as street-smart and proletarian as Spencer's is staidly traditional. In fact, the vibrant cadence and daring language of Helene Johnson's verse is reminiscent of Langston Hughes, writing, as she did, in the vernacular of Harlem street life and striking original metaphorical notes. In "Poem," for example, she boldly flirts with the subject of her mind's eye: "Gee, boy, I love the way you hold your head, / High sort of and a bit to one side, / . . . Gee, brown boy, I loves you all over. / . . . I'm glad I can / Understand your dancin' and your / Singin', and feel all the happiness / And joy and don't care in you." Her best poem, "Bottled," recapitulates the fractured grammar of everyday talk while reclaiming the derogatory epithets of racists. Indeed, the thrust of the poem is a turning-inside-out of racism. The speaker, to mention one example, sees Black people in a positive light once she stops identifying with white culture:

And yesterday on Seventh Avenue
I saw a darky dressed to kill
In yellow gloves and swallowtail coat
And swirling a cane. And everyone
Was laughing at him. Me too,
At first, till I saw his face
When he stopped to hear a
Organ grinder grind out some jazz.
Boy! You should a seen that darky's face!
It just shone. Gee, he was happy!
And he began to dance. No
Charleston or Black Bottom for him.
No sir. He danced just as dignified
And slow. No, not slow either.
Dignified and *proud*! You couldn't
Call it slow, not with all the
Cuttin' up he did. You would a died to see him.

The radical nature of this poetry lies not only in its employ of what was considered nonpoetic language, but also in Johnson's praise of those aspects of Black culture most despised by whites. She loved insouciance, sensuality, vivacity, and celebrated them. She also made clear her preference for Black American and African life over what she presented as the oppressive qualities of white ways. "Bottled" compares a geological specimen of brown sand collected from the Sahara desert to the dancing man on Seventh Avenue, declaring that he, like it, was stolen, labelled, and put on display for the enjoyment of his captors. His African roots are recalled in the speaker's imagination as she restores to him the splendor of an environment that does not denigrate Black people, one that is compatible with his spontaneity. Similarly, in "Magalu," the speaker warns a young African woman not to be seduced by a missionary to whom she is eagerly listening:

Do not let him lure you from your laughing waters,
Lulling lakes, lissome winds.
Would you sell the colors of your sunset and the fragrance
Of your flowers, and the passionate wonder of your forest
For a creed that will not let you dance?

Johnson's imagination was clearly activated by the sights and sounds of jazz age Harlem. Whenever she strays from that idiom, her writing tends to be flat, labored, inauthentic. Although she could compose competent lyric verse, it neither sings nor moves the heart. She produced very little of the avant-garde poetry on which she could have established a considerable literary reputation, however.

Helene Johnson belonged to the inner circle of renegade artists who brought to life experimental periodicals such as *Fire!!* and contributed to every major anthology and journal of her day, but, in spite of her talent and energy, she virtually disappeared from the historical record.[67] We know Johnson was born in 1907 and raised in Boston, attended Boston University, and entered Columbia in 1926. She evidently moved back to Boston in the late twenties, where she joined a group of young Black intellectuals who started a literary journal called *The Saturday Evening Quill*.[68] She last appears in print in March 1934 when friend and editor Dorothy West published her work in the Boston journal, *Challenge*.[69] Arna Bontemps reported, in the late sixties, that Johnson was living in Brooklyn with her husband and two children, and no death date has been recorded. No one seems to know what happened to her after the Renaissance ended.[70] The literary fate of this promising poet is instructive, for it underscores the invisible forces operating against distinctive female voices from the twenties. Even with an excellent ear, disciplined writing, and far-reaching social connections, Helene Johnson could not survive the era that inspired her.

Mae Cowdery, like Johnson, hit the New York scene at a very young age, captured the attention of prominent scholars and editors, and then vanished. She was one of the few women to publish a volume of verse, in which she included love poems to women.[71] The only child of a prosperous Philadelphia caterer and social worker, Cowdery gravitated quickly to the Greenwich Village crowd when she arrived in New York after graduating from high school in 1927, by which early age she had already won first prize in a poetry contest run by *The Crisis*. Her writing reportedly was heavily influenced by Edna St. Vincent Millay, and she is said to have worn tailored suits, bow ties, and kept her short hair "slicked down to patent leather."[72]

This arresting personal portrait is enough to attract the attention of modern readers, but it is Cowdery's writing that proves most compelling. Her forte was the poetry of passion, anguished, fierce, and erotic. While much of her work is clumsy, there is a spark of originality that makes it stand out from other poetry of her day, a modern quality of spareness and physical directness. She refers, for instance, to her speaker's "lust," "tempestuous ardor," and "carnal anticipation" in "Lines to a Sophisticate." The speaker assures her lover that she does not want to possess but to "savor and sip slowly / That I might know each separate scent / Of your elusive fragrance." "Insatiate" examines a lesbian's contradictory feelings about sexual infidelity, and her speaker longs for a lost lover's touch in "Farewell," moaning: "No more / The feel of your hand / On my breast / Like the silver path / Of the moon / On dark heaving ocean." The personae of her poems gaze upon lovers with open desire, recall exquisite moments of intimacy, and indulge themselves in the heat of passion, as in "Exultation" where the speaker shouts: "O night! / With stars burning— / Fire falling / Into a dark and whispering sea!"

This was unusually frank poetry for the 1920s, and it is remarkable that Cowdery published as much as she did, perhaps suggesting with what receptivity lyric poets were greeted. Though her output was impressive, the content of more than passing interest, and her aesthetic decidedly modern, today's readers know nothing of Mae Cowdery's work.[73] This is partly explained by her omission from most of the period's anthologies, which were published when she was still a high school student in Philadelphia, and partly by the fact that her collection of mainly twenties material did not appear until 1936 and so does not seem to be a product of the Harlem Renaissance. In addition, she seems to have been curiously distant from other Black women poets, who tended to know each other, and so is not mentioned in their personal papers. Dependent on men for visibility (most notably William S. Braithwaite, Langston Hughes, and Arthur Huff Fauset), Cowdery possibly arrived on the Harlem literary scene too late to forge the links with other women that might have at least marked her as one of the era's promising women writers for future readers and, more poignantly, that might have saved her life (she died by suicide in 1953).

Cowdery's invisibility, the silencing of Helene Johnson's remarkable voice, and Anne Spencer's failure to publish after 1931 suggest to us how women poets, who played such a key role in the Harlem Renaissance, disappeared not only from popular but from historical view. All Black writers suffered from the impact of the Depression on the publishing industry, of course, and the proletarian sensibility of the 1930s was out of tune with the jazz age rhythms and romantic leanings of twenties poetry. Nevertheless, women endured greater reverses than the men in their subsequent scholarly treatment, which, in part, illustrates how dependent they were on male mentors who understood and shared in their poetic vision. Once the male scholars of their generation left the scene, they had no advocates. This, combined with their failure to leave many published collections, made them vulnerable to later sexist appraisals of their part in this historic cultural movement.

Moreover, we can see from the fact that most women stopped writing after 1931 that the existence of a female support system was crucial for their work as well. The community that pulled together women from Philadelphia, Boston, New York, Washington D.C., and small towns began to disintegrate toward the end of the decade when several got married, moved, or experienced personal losses.[74] In addition, important gatekeepers disappeared at this time when Jessie Fauset left *The Crisis*, where she had been literary editor for many years, and Gwendolyn Bennett was forced out of her teaching post at Howard University, subsequently stepping down as assistant editor at *Opportunity*.[75] There were those who went against this trend, such as Georgia Douglas Johnson and Alice Dunbar-Nelson, who wrote until the end of their lives, but even they favored prose over poetry thereafter. Although not always in positions to further each other's careers, women poets received emotional support from socializing together, reviewing each other's work, and having female role models. All these things helped them deal with the pressures that flowed from being a Black woman artist. We can speculate that, once this fragile network fell apart, they had a hard time holding on to their identities as writers.

Finally, it is clear that the New Negro Movement was male-dominated, both in terms of access to resources and the kind of writing that garnered the highest praise. One has only to compare the exuberant writing of Claude McKay and Langston Hughes as they rambled through Europe with the frightened, homesick diary entries of Gwendolyn Bennett in Paris to get a glimpse of how problematic bohemian adventure was for women.[76] And sexual sophistication and international travel distinguished Harlem Renaissance artists from the previous generation. Women were largely excluded from these experiences which hurt their artistic careers.[77] In addition, there is plenty of evidence that the close personal ties of male writers to Alain Locke gave them an inside track for acquiring grants and other aids.[78] Anne Spencer, for example, reported that she was held back by Locke because he wanted to promote Countée Cullen.[79] Even though some men were supportive of women's writing, the lion's share of attention went to other men, which established a historical trajectory not easily reversed.

When measured against the historical role Renaissance artists claimed for themselves as creators of a new Afro-American sensibility, much of their work apparently fails. Nathan Huggins, for example, considers Claude McKay and Countée Cullen flawed poets because they embraced a European artistic tradition at odds with their own experience. Crippled by their notion that art should be universal, and not focus on race alone, and unable or unwilling to depart from traditional structures, they fell short of the greatness they sought.[80] J. Saunders Redding also faults Cullen for being inhibited by verse modeled after nineteenth-century Romantic lyricists and concludes he contributed little to Afro-American literature, standing aloof as he did from revolutionary currents of his time.[81] Finally, in his discussion of Renaissance novelists, Addison Gayle, Jr., concludes that Black writers were not able fully to develop their questioning and rebellious vision because they were limited by white patronage.[82] All of these things can be said of women as well, with the additional constraints imposed by a male-dominated setting. Their failure to challenge a literary tradition built by the very culture that oppressed them resulted in a rather awkward fusion of radical sentiment and sentimental form, just as the movement toward affirming things distinctly Afro-American conflicted with an impulse to define their sensibility in Romantic or classical terms. In many ways, these poets failed to provide the kind of legacy they aspired to create, and the contradictions under which they labored produced, at times, curiously stilted pieces.

Yet, although much of women's poetry is clichéd, there is a body of work that speaks with a distinctly modern cadence, artfully expressing messages of substance. Poems of high aesthetic quality were left to us by Anne Spencer, Angelina Weld Grimké, Gwendolyn Bennett, Mae Cowdery, and Helene Johnson who collectively helped expand the boundaries of poetry to include Imagism, blank verse, and the Afro-American oral tradition. Moreover, Georgia Douglas Johnson and Effie Lee Newsome were solid composers of popular verse, an important component of any progressive movement.

We can see today the class bias that kept most women from exploring the new frontiers being opened up by Langston Hughes and Zora Neale Hurston, but, if we are to comprehend the sensibility of these poets, we must be sensitive to the difficulties under which they wrote and the historical conditions that shaped their thinking. As women, they were comfortable with the arena of private poetry, and it reflects the circumscribed conditions in which they lived. Gloria Hull has pointed out that role expectations inhibited female writers from the boldness that characterizes the most experimental literature of the day.[83] It is possible to see them remaining within a female as well as a white tradition, therefore, as they explored their inner selves, intimate relations with lovers, and private connections to the natural world. They found congenial poetic models in the Imagists and English Romantics because these forms allowed them access to a core self. Communing with nature in spontaneous, associative ways or unself-consciously exploring the intensity of their most intimate connections with lovers furnished a markedly female strategy for claiming an Afro-American worldview.

The current revival of interest in women writers from this pivotal era is revising our notion of what the Harlem Renaissance was all about. The debt modern Black writers owe to these pioneers of self-expression is increasingly being recognized. Gloria Hull, for instance, concludes that contemporary Afro-American women writers have been able to achieve a liberating, self-oriented perspective, in part because their forerunners adopted the "lyric 'I' persona."[84] Likewise, Bernard Bell credits the lyricism of the New Negro movement with stimulating a similar artistic awakening among Third World writers.[85] It may be that the way in which Renaissance poets will prove most influential is the road they paved toward a distinctly twentieth-century sensibility based on intimacy, frank espousal of feelings, and the search for personal empowerment in a world intent on denying Black people their humanity. If so, we will come to see these poets as the daring people they were, appropriating a cultural heritage they were told was beyond their grasp, and blazing a path for those who would follow.

NOTES TO INTRODUCTION

1. Studies that omit women altogether include J. Saunders Redding, *To Make a Poet Black* (Chapel Hill: University of North Carolina Press, 1939); Blyden Jackson and Louis Rubin, eds., *Black Poetry in America* (Baton Rouge: Louisiana State University Press, 1974); Jean Wagner, *Black Poets of the United States* (Urbana: University of Illinois Press, 1973); and Wallace Thurman, "Negro Poets and Their Poetry" in *Black Expression: Essays By and About Black Americans in the Creative Arts*, ed. Addison Gayle, Jr., (New York: Weybright & Talley, 1969). Arthur P. Davis, *From the Dark Tower: Afro-American Writers, 1900–1960* (Washington, D.C.: Howard University Press, 1974) discusses women fiction writers but no poets; Arthur P. Davis and J. Saunders Redding, eds., *Cavalcade: Negro American Writing from 1760 to the Present* (Boston: Houghton Mifflin, 1971) include two women poets, Frances E. W. Harper and Anne Spencer.

2. Sterling Brown, *Negro Poetry and Drama* (Washington, D.C.: Associations in Negro Folk Education, 1937), pp. 62 and 65. See also Benjamin Brawley, *The Negro in Literature and Art in the United States.* (New York: Duffield & Co., 1930), pp. 111–113. James Weldon Johnson, ed., *The Book of American Negro Poetry* (1931; reprint, New York: Harcourt, Brace, and World, 1959), pp. 243 and 205. Other anthologies that include significant numbers of women from this period are Countée Cullen, ed., *Caroling Dusk: An Anthology of Verse by Negro Poets* (1927; reprint, New York: Harper & Row, 1955); V. F. Calverton, ed., *Anthology of American Negro Literature* (New York: The Modern Library, 1929); William S. Braithwaite, ed., *Anthology of Magazine Verse for 1928* (New York: Harold Vinal, 1928); and Robert T. Kerlin, ed., *Negro Poets and Their Poems* (Washington, D.C.: Associated Publishers, 1923).

3. Margaret Perry, *Silence to the Drums: A Survey of the Literature of the Harlem Renaissance* (Westport, CT: Greenwood Press, 1976), p. 153; Margaret Just Butcher, *The Negro in American Culture* (New York: Alfred A. Knopf, 1973), p. 123.

4. Arthur P. Davis and Michael Peplow, eds., *The New Negro Renaissance: An Anthology* (New York: Harper & Row, 1975) place poems by Jessie Fauset, Anne Spencer, Angelina Weld Grimké, and Georgia

Douglas Johnson under the category "Raceless Literature." See also Richard Barksdale and Keneth Kinnamon, eds., *Black Writers of America: A Comprehensive Anthology* (New York: Macmillan, 1972).

5. Omitting names whose gender was not clearly marked (e.g., first name omitted in favor of initials), a total of 347 poems appears by men in both journals from 1918 through 1931 and 277 by women. The numbers are nearly even for *The Crisis*, where Jessie Fauset was literary editor.

6. Exceptions to this trend are Davis and Peplow, eds., *The New Negro Renaissance*, who include poems by women under the category "Race Pride." Arna Bontemps, ed., *American Negro Poetry* (New York: Hill & Wang, 1963) anthologizes many women's poems concerning race; Nathan Huggins's, *Voices from the Harlem Renaissance* (New York: Oxford University Press, 1976) is another anthology with poetry of this kind; William Adams et al., eds., *Afro-American Literature* (Boston: Houghton Mifflin, 1970) reprint racial poetry by Bennett, Helene Johnson, and Frances Harper.

7. Nella Larsen, *Quicksand and Passing*, ed. Deborah McDowell (New Brunswick: Rutgers University Press, 1986) and Jessie Fauset, *Plum Bun*, ed. Deborah McDowell (1928; reprint, London: Pandora Press, 1985). Gloria Hull, *Color, Sex, and Poetry: Three Women Writers of the Harlem Renaissance* (Bloomington: Indiana University Press, 1987). Erlene Stetson, ed., *Black Sister: Poetry by Black American Women, 1746–1980* (Bloomington: Indiana University Press, 1981), p. xxii. A recent text showcasing women writers from this period is Ann Allen Shockley, ed., *Afro-American Women Writers, 1746–1933: An Anthology and Critical Guide* (Boston: G. K. Hall, 1988).

8. The selections for this anthology were culled from all the poetry by women that appears in anthologies from the 1920s and in every issue of *Opportunity* and *The Crisis* from 1918 to 1931.

9. Quoted in Carolyn Sylvander, *Jessie Redmon Fauset, Black American Writer* (Troy, NY: The Whitston Publishing Co., 1981), p. 83.

10. Cullen, *Caroling Dusk*, p. 47.

11. George Kent, "Patterns of the Harlem Renaissance," in *The Harlem Renaissance Remembered*, ed. Arna Bontemps (New York: Dodd, Mead & Co., 1972). See also Florette Henri, *Black Migration: Movement North 1900–1920* (Garden City, NY: Anchor Books, 1975). For discussion of racism during the World War I period, see Gilbert Osofsky, *Harlem: The Making of a Ghetto, Negro New York 1890–1930* (New York: Harper & Row, 1963); August Meier and Elliot Rudwick,

From Plantation to Ghetto: An Interpretive History of American Negroes (New York: Hill & Wang, 1966); and Paula Giddings, *When and Where I Enter: The Impact of Black Women on Race and Sex in America* (New York: William Morrow & Co., 1984).

12. Black women were frustrated, for instance, by the insensitivity of white feminists to their political agenda although NAWSA did condemn lynching in 1917. The racism of the Woman Movement is well documented in Erlene Stetson, "Black Feminism in Indiana, 1893–1933," *Phylon* 44 (December 1983):292–298 and Rosalyn Terborg-Penn, "Discrimination against Afro-American Women in the Women's Movement, 1830–1920," in *The Afro-American Woman: Struggles and Images*, eds. Sharon Harley and Rosalyn Terborg-Penn (Port Washington, NY: Kennikat Press, 1978).

13. Bettina Aptheker, *Woman's Legacy: Essays on Race, Sex, and Class in American History* (Amherst: University of Massachusetts Press, 1982), p. 27.

14. An exposition of this racist ideology is provided by Forrest G. Wood, *Black Scare: The Racist Response to Emancipation and Reconstruction* (Berkeley: University of California Press, 1968). See also C. Vann Woodward, *The Strange Career of Jim Crow* (New York: Oxford University Press, 1966); John Higham, *Strangers in the Land: Patterns of American Nativism, 1860–1925* (New York: Atheneum Press, 1963); Kenneth Jackson, *The Ku Klux Klan in the City, 1915–1930* (New York: Oxford University Press, 1967); and I. A. Newby, *Jim Crow's Defense: Anti-Negro Thought in America, 1900–1930* (Baton Rouge: Louisiana State University Press, 1965).

15. Nathan Huggins, *The Harlem Renaissance* (New York: Oxford University Press, 1971), p. 6.

16. The reluctance felt by many of this generation toward incorporating folk dialect, perceived as tainted by its use in plantation literature, into their art, is recorded in Johnson, *Book of American Negro Poetry*, p. 3.

17. Huggins, *Harlem Renaissance*, p. 303.

18. Ibid., p. 5. Agreeing with this perspective is Amritjit Singh, *The Novels of the Harlem Renaissance* (University Park: Pennsylvania State University Press, 1976), p. 17.

19. A good treatment of the patron roles played by whites during the Harlem Renaissance is Bruce Kellner, *Carl Van Vechten and the Irreverent Decades* (Norman: University of Oklahoma Press, 1968).

20. Good examples of such criticism are J. Saunders Redding, "The New Negro Poet in the Twenties," in *Modern Black Poets*, ed. Donald

Gibson (Englewood Cliffs, NJ: Prentice-Hall, 1973); Addison Gayle, Jr., *The Way of the New World: The Black Novel in America* (Garden City, NY: Anchor Books, 1975); and Gerald Moore, "Poetry in the Harlem Renaissance," *The Black American Writer*, Vol. 2, ed. C. W. E. Bigsby, (DeLano, FL: Everett/Edwards, 1969).

21. Hurston's conventional poetry is described in Tony Martin, *Literary Garveyism: Garvey, Black Arts, and the Harlem Renaissance* (Dover, MA: The Majority Press, 1983), pp. 73–75. In his biography of Zora Neale Hurston, Robert Hemenway describes the attitude of Renaissance artists toward Black folk culture and their aim of transforming it into "conscious art." *Zora Neale Hurston: A Literary Biography* (Urbana: University of Illinois Press, 1977), p. 62. Nathan Huggins also discusses artists' perspectives on European high art forms in *Harlem Renaissance*, pp. 161–209.

22. Elaboration on the Romantic poetic tradition these writers emulated is provided by Menna Alexander, *The Poetic Self: Towards a Phenomenology of Romanticism* (Atlantic Highlands, NJ: Humanities Press, 1980); Willis Barnstone, *The Poetics of Ecstacy: Varieties of Ekstasis from Sappho to Borges* (New York: Holmes & Meir, 1983); and M. A. Goldberg, *The Poetics of Romanticism: Toward a Reading of John Keats* (Yellow Springs, OH: Antioch Press, 1969).

23. This point is made by Gregory Holmes Singleton in "Birth, Rebirth, and the 'New Negro' of the 1920's," *Phylon* 43 (March 1982): 29–45; Singh, *Novels*, p. 22; and Wayne Cooper, "Claude McKay and the New Negro of the 1920's," in *Black American Writer*, ed. Bigsby.

24. Henry F. May describes the beginning of this movement in *The End of American Innocence: A Study of the First Years of Our Own Time, 1912–1917* (New York: Alfred A. Knopf, 1959).

25. Discussion of white fascination with Afro-Americans at this time is provided by Huggins, *Harlem Renaissance*, p. 254.

26. Houston, "Ecstasy," *The Crisis* (February 1929); Young, "Hunger," *Opportunity* (June 1928).

27. Angelina Weld Grimké stated, for instance, that her poems depended on analogues she found in nature for the concepts she was trying to express. Hull, *Color, Sex, and Poetry*, p. 24.

28. J. Lee Greene, *Time's Unfading Garden: Anne Spencer's Life and Poetry* (Baton Rouge: Louisiana State University Press, 1977), p. 130.

29. Ibid., p. 3.

30. This information was conveyed by Spencer to J. Lee Greene at the end of her life. Ibid., p. 140.

31. Blanche Taylor Dickinson, "Four Walls," in *Caroling Dusk*, ed. Cullen.

32. Ronald Primeau, "Frank Horne and the Second Echelon Poets of the Harlem Renaissance" in *The Harlem Renaissance Remembered*, ed. Bontemps.

33. Hull, *Color, Sex, and Poetry*, p. 145.

34. This view of Spencer's poetry is explicated by Greene in *Time's Unfading Garden*, pp. 99–127.

35. Helene Johnson, "What Do I Care for Morning," in *Caroling Dusk*, ed. Cullen.

36. Ethel M. Caution, "Last Night," *The Crisis* (February 1929); Marjorie Marshall, "To a Dark Dancer," *The Crisis* (January 1928); Mae V. Cowdery, "Longings," *The Crisis* (December 1927).

37. Michael Cooke, *Afro-American Literature in the Twentieth Century* (New Haven: Yale University Press, 1984), pp. 35–41.

38. For amplification on the connection between self and nature made by Romantic poets, who served as role models for Renaissance poets, see M. H. Abrams, ed., *English Romantic Poets* (New York: Oxford University Press, 1975).

39. Bernard Bell, *The Afro-American Novel and Its Tradition* (Amherst: University of Massachusetts Press, 1987), p. 114.

40. See Huggins, *Harlem Renaissance*, pp. 244–301, and Osofsky, *Making of a Ghetto*, p. 184, on the psychological importance of such a caricature for whites.

41. Joan Sherman, ed., *Invisible Poets: Afro-Americans of the Nineteenth Century* (Urbana: University of Illinois Press, 1974), p. xxi.

42. Lindsay Patterson, ed., *A Rock Against the Wind: Black Love Poems* (New York: Dodd, Mead & Co., 1973), p. xiii.

43. A description of this stereotype appears in Thomas Cripps, *Slow Fade to Black: The Negro in American Film, 1900–1942* (New York: Oxford University Press, 1977).

44. Alain Locke, ed., *The New Negro: An Interpretation* (New York: Albert and Charles Boni, 1925).

45. Singleton, "Birth, Rebirth."

46. Given the closeted existence of lesbians in the early twentieth century, it is difficult to identify them. It is clear, however, that some poets who were single wrote poems that suggest they were attracted to women. These would include Angelina Weld Grimké, Mae V. Cowdery, and Gladys Mae Casely Hayford. Both Alice Dunbar-Nelson and Anne Spencer were married, but they lived with female relatives who relieved them of many household responsibilities, allowing them to

write and do political work. Jessie Fauset and Gwendolyn Bennett did not marry until the end of the decade. Helene Johnson remained single throughout this period.

47. Lillian Faderman, *Surpassing the Love of Men: Romantic Friendship and Love between Women from the Renaissance to the Present* (New York: William Morrow & Co., 1981).

48. Gloria Hull, ed., *Give Us Each Day: The Diary of Alice Dunbar-Nelson* (New York: W. W. Norton, 1984) and "'Under the Days': The Buried Life and Poetry of Angelina Weld Grimké," *Conditions* 2 (Autumn 1979): 17–25.

49. Gloria Hull discusses the sexual preference of both these men in *Color, Sex, and Poetry*, p. 8.

50. This anthology remains one of the best resources for studying poetry by women of the Harlem Renaissance, including, as it does, every major female writer except Mae Cowdery, whose career was just starting when it appeared.

51. One critic, for example, has called Cullen, "a gentle, schoolroom poet" whose poetry is "effete" and "bloodless": "It is as if he saw life through the eyes of a woman." Redding, "New Negro Poet."

52. Locke's, Cullen's, and Hughes's sexual preference has been unacknowledged until recently and its complex impact on the careers of women is only now being explored.

53. Georgia Douglas Johnson, *An Autumn Love Cycle* (1928; reprint, Freeport, NY: Books for Libraries Press, 1971), p. xviii.

54. Vincent Jubilee, "Philadelphia's Afro-American Literary Circle and the Harlem Renaissance" (Ph.D. diss., University of Pennsylvania, 1980), p. 65.

55. Literature on Black gay and lesbian life in the twenties includes Eric Garber, "Gladys Bentley: The Bulldagger Who Sang the Blues," *Outlook* 1 (Spring 1988): 52–61; Sandra Lieb, *Mother of the Blues: A Study of Ma Rainey* (Amherst: University of Massachusetts Press, 1981); Chris Albertson, *Bessie* (New York: Stein & Day, 1972).

56. Hull, *Color, Sex, and Poetry*, pp. 9, 11, 187.

57. Lillian Faderman discusses this homophobic reaction as a backlash against women's rights in *Surpassing*, pp. 231–294.

58. Those who divide Harlem writers into bourgeois and radical groups include Gayle, *Way of the New World*, and Robert Bone, *The Negro Novel in America* (New Haven: Yale University Press, 1965).

59. All biographical information on Anne Spencer is taken from Greene, *Time's Unfading Garden*.

60. Ibid., p. 20.

61. Ibid., p. 3.

62. Ibid., pp. 136–137.

63. Ibid., p. 141.

64. Ibid., pp. 134 and 148.

65. Ibid., pp. 129 and 140.

66. Hull, *Color, Sex, and Poetry*.

67. This circle included Langston Hughes, Zora Neale Hurston, Gwendolyn Bennett, Wallace Thurman, Dorothy West, and Alain Locke, among others.

68. This periodical was published from 1928 until 1930.

69. *Challenge* spans the years 1934–1937.

70. Addison Gayle, Jr., ed., *Black Expression*.

71. Cowdery, *We Lift Our Voices*. William Stanley Braithwaite wrote an introduction for this volume.

72. Bruce Kellner, ed., *The Harlem Renaissance: An Annotated Bibliography* (Westport, CT: Greenwood Press, 1984), p. 84. Biographical information is from Jubilee, "Philadelphia's Afro-American Literary Circle," pp. 59–69.

73. The exception is Erlene Stetson, who reprints one of Cowdery's poems in *Black Sister*.

74. Jessie Fauset married Herbert Harris in 1929; Gwendolyn Bennett married a medical student at Howard and moved to Florida with him in 1927; Angelina Weld Grimké was traumatized by the death of her father in 1930 and went into seclusion in New York City; and Clarissa Scott Delany, a close friend of Grimké's, died in 1927.

75. On Jessie Fauset's key role in the Harlem Renaissance, see Abby Arthur Johnson, "Literary Midwife: Jessie Redmon Fauset and the Harlem Renaissance," *Phylon* 39 (June 1978):143–153; and Deborah McDowell, "The Neglected Dimension of Jessie Fauset," in *Conjuring: Black Women, Fiction, and the Literary Tradition*, ed. Hortense Spillers and Marjorie Pryse (Bloomington: University of Indiana Press, 1985).

76. Personal papers of Gwendolyn Bennett (Box 1, Folder 1), The New York Public Library, Schomberg Center for Research in Black Culture, New York City.

77. Nathan Huggins explores the macho dimension of Renaissance bohemianism in *Harlem Renaissance*, pp. 188–200.

78. Hull, *Color, Sex, and Poetry*, pp. 7–10.

79. Greene, *Time's Unfading Garden*, p. 140.

80. Huggins, *Harlem Renaissance*, pp. 161–214.

81. Redding, "New Negro Poet."

82. Gayle, *Way of the New World*, pp. 5, 95, 107.

83. Hull believes the privileging of male writers in the Harlem Renaissance had a disastrous impact on women. *Color, Sex, and Poetry*, pp. 7–25.

84. Hull, *Color, Sex, and Poetry*, p. 215. Barbara Christian similarly believes that modern Black female writers are characterized by self-exploration. *Black Woman Novelists: The Development of a Tradition, 1892–1976* (Westport, CT: Greenwood Press, 1980), p. 246.

85. Bell, *Afro-American Novel*, p. 116. See also Michael Cooke, who says focus on the inner life distinguishes the most recent phase of Black American literature (*Afro-American Literature*, p. 41).

A Note on the Text

The poems for this anthology were culled from all the poetry published by Black women in the organs of the New Negro movement, *Opportunity* and *The Crisis*, between the years 1918, when Georgia Douglas Johnson published her first volume of verse, and 1931, the last year in which large numbers of poems by women appear. Established in 1910 by the NAACP and run by W. E. B. DuBois, *The Crisis* reached a circulation of 95,000 by 1919 and is widely credited with spearheading the Renaissance movement. *Opportunity* was created by the Urban League in 1923, was headed by Charles S. Johnson, and enjoyed a circulation of 11,000 by 1927. Both magazines devoted much space in each issue to literary material, while fostering newly emerging Black writers through poetry, fiction, and essay contests. Anthologies and collections from the period furnished the other poems included here. All publication dates within the period have been included to indicate how well distributed any given poem was. The only changes that have been made to the original pieces are corrections of typographical, spelling, and punctuation errors and lengthening of lines that were obviously limited by the width of the columns in the journals.

The selection process was governed by a number of factors. One of these was that I wanted to represent all the major poets with a good number of pieces, their lesser known works as well as those that have been reprinted, in order to give a sense of their range. I felt it was important, too, to include writers who never made it into anthologies. Most women had neither the resources nor the social contacts to compile a significant body of work, yet they played a key role in the cultural awakening of the 1920s and suggest its broadly based nature. Another determinant of whether a given poem would be included was its artistic value. Admittedly relying on subjective judgment, I looked for pieces that have held up over time and that contain striking metaphors or well-composed lines to underscore the contemporary, as well as historical, value of this poetry. I eliminated, for instance, verse that seemed to me derivative or awkwardly rendered. Finally, I chose poems representative of the subjects and themes that appear most frequently during this period and provide a glimpse into the concerns and sensibility of the Renaissance generation. Most women's poetry fell into the four categories that appear here: Protest, Heritage, Love and Passion, and Nature. Rather than group the pieces by poet, an appealing arrangement that I abandoned with some reluctance, I chose to present them within these categories in order to highlight a revealing consistency of theme and metaphor. To that end, as well, I arranged poems by author within each section but ordered them according to subject to underscore this thematic continuity. These poems reverberate with notes commonly struck and their meaning is enriched by the threads that weave them together. This literary generation shared a voice as well as a historical era.

At the same time, individuals created their own unique style and so I have grouped the poems by writer within each category. Each section begins with a major figure to recognize her achievements. Anne Spencer heads the collection as she has been reprinted the most often and because, ironically (since her reputation is that of a pastoralist), it is her work that is the most overtly political. Beginning the Heritage section is Helene Johnson, whose innovative language and nonbourgeois subjects put her in the forefront of those seeking to create a modern Black aesthetic. The third part, Love and Passion, is led by a little-known poet named Mae V. Cowdery. Her large output, daring poetic forays into erotic love for other women, and association with leading intellectuals of her day qualify her, in my mind, as a pivotal artist. Finally, the imagist portraits of Angelina Weld Grimké and a moving poem by Alice Dunbar-Nelson introduce the nature poetry they and so many other women found attractive. Gwendolyn B. Bennett, poet, painter, editor, and college professor, ends the collection. I have chosen her "Street Lamps in Early Spring" as the final poem because it symbolizes for me the affirmative spirit of the Harlem Renaissance and captures writers' attempts to give birth to a new identity. At the same time, Bennett veils the Black goddess in her poem, just as this poetry has been veiled, hidden in shadows, kept alive by dreams.

ONE

Protest

White Things

ANNE SPENCER

Most things are colorful things—the sky, earth, and sea.
  Black men are most men; but the white are free!
White things are rare things; so rare, so rare
They stole from out a silvered world—somewhere.
Finding earth-plains fair plains, save greenly grassed,
They strewed white feathers of cowardice, as they passed;
  The golden stars with lances fine,
  The hills all red and darkened pine,
They blanched with their wand of power;
And turned the blood in a ruby rose
To a poor white poppy-flower.

They pyred a race of black, black men,
And burned them to ashes white; then,
Laughing, a young one claimed a skull,
For the skull of a black is white, not dull,
  But a glistening awful thing
  Made, it seems, for this ghoul to swing
In the face of God with all his might,
And swear by the hell that sired him:
  "Man-maker, make white!"

From *The Crisis* (March 1923)

The Sévignés

Down in Natchitoches there is a statue in a public square
A slave replica—not of Uncle Tom, praise God,
But of Uncle Remus . . . a big plinth holding a little
    man bowing humbly to a master-mistress
This shameless thing set up to the intricate involvement
    of human slavery.
Go, see it, read it, with whatever heart you have left.
No penance, callous beyond belief.
For these women who had so lately fled from the
    slavery of Europe to the great wilds of America.

(unpublished)

Letter to My Sister

ANNE SPENCER

It is dangerous for a woman to defy the gods;
To taunt them with the tongue's thin tip,
Or strut in the weakness of mere humanity,
Or draw a line daring them to cross;
The gods own the searing lightning,
The drowning waters, tormenting fears
And anger of red sins.

Oh, but worse still if you mince timidly—
Dodge this way or that, or kneel or pray,
Be kind, or sweat agony drops
Or lay your quick body over your feeble young;
If you have beauty or none, if celibate
Or vowed—the gods are Juggernaut,
Passing over . . . over . . .

This you may do:
Lock your heart, then, quietly,
And lest they peer within,
Light no lamp when dark comes down
Raise no shade for sun;
Breathless must your breath come through
If you'd die and dare deny
The gods their god-like fun.

From *Ebony and Topaz*, ed. Charles S. Johnson (1927)

Innocence

ANNE SPENCER

She tripped and fell against a star,
A lady we all have known;
Just what the villagers lusted for
To claim her one of their own;
Fallen but, once, the lower fell she,
So turned her face and died,—
With never a hounding fool to see
'Twas a star-lance in her side!

From *Caroling Dusk*, ed. Countée Cullen (1927)

Before the Feast at Shushan

ANNE SPENCER

Garden of Shushan!
After Eden, all terrace, pool, and flower recollect thee:
Ye weaves in saffron and haze and Tyrian purple,
Tell yet what range in color wakes the eye;
Sorcerer, release the dreams born here when
Drowsy, shifting palm-shade enspells the brain;
And sound! ye with harp and flute ne'er essay
Before these star-noted birds escaped from paradise awhile to
Stir all dark, and dear, and passionate desire, till mine
Arms go out to be mocked by the softly kissing body of the
    wind—
Slave, send Vashti to her King!

The fiery wattles of the sun startle into flame
The marbled towers of Shushan:
So at each day's wane, two peers—the one in
Heaven, the other on earth—welcome with their
Splendor the peerless beauty of the Queen.

Cushioned at the Queen's feet and upon her knee
Finding glory for mine head,—still, nearly shamed
Am I, the King, to bend and kiss with sharp
Breath the olive-pink of sandaled toes between;
Or lift me high to the magnet of a gaze, dusky,
Like the pool when but the moon-ray strikes to its depth;
Or closer press to crush a grape 'gainst lips redder
Than the grape, a rose in the night of her hair;
Then—Sharon's Rose in my arms.

And I am hard to force the petals wide;
And you are fast to suffer and be sad.
Is any prophet come to teach a new thing
Now in a more apt time?
Have him 'maze how you say love is sacrament;

How, says Vashti, love is both bread and wine;
How to the altar may not come to break and drink,
Hulky flesh nor fleshly spirit!

I, thy lord, like not manna for meat as a Judahn;
I, thy master, drink, and red wine, plenty, and when
I thirst. Eat meat, and full, when I hunger.
I, thy King, teach you and leave you, when I list.
No woman in all Persia sets out strange action
To confuse Persia's lord—
Love is but desire and thy purpose fulfillment;
I, thy King, so say!

From *The Crisis* (February 1920); *The Book of American Negro
Poetry*, ed. James Weldon Johnson (1031)

[Terence MacSwiney]

ANNE SPENCER

Terence MacSwiney
In days gone by many an Irish lad, had I called you,
would have answered "I am here," for yours was only
a name to live by.
You raced with the wind along your glittering shore
Woke at dawn
Slept at dawn
Ate what food
Drank what drink
Warmed by peat as you breathed it.
That was a boy's day
But one day you slept too long—
When you awoke you were a man—in a land you never saw
      before
Rightly nor had you known before the whole state
Stone on stone to house the rich,
Hovel on hovel to cover the poor.
Talk is as the wind. What?
I have something—I can lay it down, I can take it up again.
This I do for Erin, my beloved land.
Terence, Terence in glory forever,
Now lovers have another name to die by.

(unpublished)

Lady, Lady

ANNE SPENCER

Lady, Lady, I saw your face,
Dark as night withholding a star . . .
The chisel fell, or it might have been
You had borne so long the yoke of men.
Lady, Lady, I saw your hands,
Twisted, awry, like crumpled roots,
Bleached poor white in a sudsy tub,
Wrinkled and drawn from your rub-a-dub.
Lady, Lady, I saw your heart,
And altared there in its darksome place
Were the tongues of flames the ancients knew,
Where the good God sits to spangle through.

From *Survey* (March 1925); *The New Negro*,
ed. Alain Locke (1925)

Prejudice

GEORGIA DOUGLAS JOHNSON

These fell miasmic rings of mist with ghoulish menace bound,
Like noose-horizons tightening my little world around.
They still the soaring will to wing, to dance, to speed away,
And fling the soul insurgent back into its shell of clay.
Beneath incrusted silences, a seething Etna lies,
The fire of whose furnaces may sleep, but never dies!

From *Bronze: A Book of Verse* (1922)

Common Dust

GEORGIA DOUGLAS JOHNSON

And who shall separate the dust
What later we shall be:
Whose keen discerning eye will scan
And solve the mystery?

The high, the low, the rich, the poor,
The black, the white, the red,
And all the chromatique between,
Of whom shall it be said:

Here lies the dust of Africa;
Here are the sons of Rome;
Here lies the one unlabelled,
The world at large his home!

Can one then separate the dust?
Will mankind lie apart,
When life has settled back again
The same as from the start?

From *Bronze: A Book of Verse* (1922)

Calling Dreams

GEORGIA DOUGLAS JOHNSON

The right to make my dreams come true,
I ask, nay, I demand of life;
Nor shall fate's deadly contraband
Impede my steps, nor countermand;
Too long my heart against the ground
Has beat the dusty years around;
And now at length I rise! I wake!
And stride into the morning break!

From *The Crisis* (January 1920)

Wishes

GEORGIA DOUGLAS JOHNSON

I'm tired of pacing the petty round of the ring of the thing I
  know—
I want to stand on the daylight's edge and see where the sunsets
  go.

I want to sail on a swallow's tail and peep through the sky's blue
  glass.
I want to see if the dreams in me shall perish or come to pass.

I want to look through the moon's pale crook and gaze on the
  moon-man's face.
I want to keep all the tears I weep and sail to some unknown
  place.

From *The Crisis* (April 1927)

The Suppliant

GEORGIA DOUGLAS JOHNSON

Long have I beat with timid hands upon life's leaden door,
Praying the patient, futile prayer my fathers prayed before;
Yet I remain without the close, unheeded and unheard,
And never to my listening ear is borne the waited word.

Soft o'er the threshold of the years there comes this counsel
    cool:
The strong demand, contend, prevail; the beggar is a fool!

From *Caroling Dusk*, ed. Countée Cullen (1927)

Armageddon

GEORGIA DOUGLAS JOHNSON

In the silence and the dark
I fought with dragons:
I was battered, beaten, sore,

But rose again.
On my knees I fought, still rising,
Dull with pain!

In the dark I fought with dragons—
Foolish tears! Cease your flowing!
Can't you see the dawn appears?

From *The Crisis* (March 1925)

Your World

GEORGIA DOUGLAS JOHNSON

Your world is as big as you make it.
I know, for I used to abide
In the narrowest nest in a corner,
My wings pressing close to my side.

But I sighted the distant horizon
Where the skyline encircled the sea
And I throbbed with a burning desire
To travel this immensity.

I battered the cordons around me
And cradled my wings on the breeze,
Then soared to the uttermost reaches
With rapture, with power, with ease!

From *Bronze: A Book of Verse* (1922)

Motherhood

GEORGIA DOUGLAS JOHNSON

Don't knock on my door, little child,
I cannot let you in;
You know not what a world this is
Of cruelty and sin.
Wait in the still eternity
Until I come to you.
The world is cruel, cruel, child,
I cannot let you through.

Don't knock at my heart, little one,
I cannot bear the pain
Of turning deaf ears to your call,
Time and time again.
You do not know the monster men
Inhabiting the earth.
Be still, be still, my precious child,
I cannot give you birth.

From *The Crisis* (October 1922)

Smothered Fires

GEORGIA DOUGLAS JOHNSON

A woman with a burning flame
  Deep covered through the years
With ashes—ah! she hid it deep,
  And smothered it with tears.

Sometimes a baleful light would rise
  From out the dusky bed,
And then the woman hushed it quick
  To slumber on, as dead.

At last the weary war was done,
  The tapers were alight,
And with a sigh of victory
  She breathed a soft—goodnight!

From *The Heart of a Woman and Other Poems* (1918); *Negro Poets and Their Poems*, ed. Robert T. Kerlin (1923); *The Book of American Negro Poetry*, ed. James Weldon Johnson (1931)

The Heart of a Woman

GEORGIA DOUGLAS JOHNSON

The heart of a woman goes forth with the dawn
As a lone bird, soft winging, so restlessly on;
Afar o'er life's turrets and vales does it roam
In the wake of those echoes the heart calls home.

The heart of a woman falls back with the night,
And enters some alien cage in its plight,
And tires to forget it has dreamed of the stars
While it breaks, breaks, breaks on the sheltering bars.

From *The Heart of a Woman and Other Poems* (1918);
Caroling Dusk, ed. Countée Cullen, (1927)

The Bird in the Cage

EFFIE LEE NEWSOME

I am not better than my brother over the way,
But he has a bird in the cage and I have not.
It beats its little fretted green wings
Against the wires of its prison all day long.
Backward and forward it leaps,
While summer air is tender and the shadows of leaves
Rock on the ground,
And the earth is cool and heated in spots,
And the air from rich herbage rises teeming,
And gold of suns spills all around,

And birds within the maples
And birds upon the oaks fly and sing and flutter.
And there is that little green prisoner,
Tossing its body forward and up,
Backward and forth mechanically!
I listen for its hungry little song,
Which comes unsatisfying,
Like drops of dew dispelled by drought.
O, rosebud doomed to ripen in a bud vase!
O, bird of song within that binding cage!
Nay, I am not better than my brother over the way,
Only he has a bird in a cage and I have not.

From *The Crisis* (February 1927)

The Baker's Boy

MARY EFFIE LEE NEWSOME

The baker's boy delivers loaves
All up and down our street.
His car is white, his clothes are white,
White to his very feet.
I wonder if he stays that way.

I don't see how he does all day.
I'd like to watch him going home
When all the loaves are out.
His clothes must look quite different then,
At least I have no doubt.

From *Caroling Dusk*, ed. Countée Cullen (1927)

Exodus

EFFIE LEE NEWSOME

Rank fennel and broom
Grow wanly beside
The cottage and room
We once occupied,
But sold for the snows!

The dahoon berry weeps in blood,
I know,
Watched by the crow—
I've seen both grow
In those weird wastes of Dixie!

From *The Crisis* (January 1925)

Northboun'

LUCY ARIEL WILLIAMS

O' de wurl' ain't flat,
An' de wurl' ain't roun',
H'its one long strip
Hangin' up an' down—
Jes' Souf an' Norf;
Jes' Norf an' Souf.

Talkin' 'bout sailin' 'round de wurl'—
Huh! I'd be so dizzy my head 'ud twurl.
If dis heah earf wuz jes' a ball
You know the people all 'ud fall.

O' de wurl' ain't flat,
An' de wurl' ain't roun',
H'its one long strip
Hangin' up an' down—
Jes' Souf an' Norf;
Jes' Norf an' Souf.

Talkin' 'bout the City whut Saint John saw—
Chile, you oughta go to Saginaw;
A nigger's chance is "finest kind,"
An' pretty gals ain't hard to find.

Huh! de wurl' ain't flat,
An' de wurl' ain't roun',
Jes' one long strip
Hangin' up an' down—
Since Norf is up,
An' Souf is down,
An' Hebben is up,
I'm upward boun'.

From *Opportunity* (June 1926); *Caroling Dusk*, ed. Countée
Cullen (1927); *The Book of American Negro Poetry*,
ed. James Weldon Johnson (1931)

"Carry Me Back to Old Virginny"

ELMA EHRLICH LEVINGER

That's right: keep on singing, *"Carry Me Back to Old*
  Virginny."
I ain't heard it since Miss Lucy's little girl used to sing it,
In the parlor, when I took mamma's washing 'round the back
  way:
It's a fine song—for white folks.

"There's where the birds warble sweet in the springtime."
That's when it used to stink most down in nigger town;
We slept six in a room and the drains never worked right;
Lots of scarlet fever on account of them drains,
But folks got to expect it;
My little sister, she died of it in the springtime.

"There's where I labored so hard for old Massa."
And he took his shotgun to me once and run me off the place,
When I argued about the price he give me for my cotton;
My buddy, Jake Stone, who went to France with me, talked too
  big:
They got Jake one night over by the creek . . .
I ain't goin' to forget in a hurry what they done to him.

"No place on earth do I love more sincerely
Than old Virginny, the place where I was born—"
It's a fine place—for white folks:
But you'd have to carry me to get me back there.

From *The Crisis* (March 1924)

Crowded Out

ROSALIE M. JONAS

Nobody ain't Christmas shoppin'
Fur *his* stockin'!
Nobody ain't cotch no Tukkey,
Nobody ain't bake no pie,
Nobody's laid nuthin' by;
"Santy" ain't got nothin' hid
Fur his Mammy's little kid.

Seem like eve'body rushin'
An'er crushin',
Crowdin' shops an' jammin' trolleys,
Buyin' shoes an' shirts an' toys
Fur de *white* folks' girls an' boys,
But no hobby-horse ain't rockin'
By *his* little wore-out stockin'.

He ain't quar'lin', recollec',
He don't spec'
Nuthin'—hits his not expectin',
Makes his Mammy wish, O Laws!
Fur a *Po Folks* Santa Claus,
Totin' *any* kind er toy
Fur his Mammy's honey-boy!

From *The Crisis* (January 1924)

Little Grey Dreams

ANGELINA WELD GRIMKÉ

Little grey dreams,
I sit at the ocean's edge,
   At the grey ocean's edge,
   With you in my lap.

I launch you, one by one,
   And one by one,
     Little grey dreams,
Under the grey, grey clouds,
Out on the grey, grey sea,
You go sailing away,
From my empty lap,
     Little grey dreams.

     Sailing! sailing!
Into the black,
At the horizon's edge.

From *Opportunity* (January 1924)

I Sit and Sew

ALICE DUNBAR-NELSON

I sit and sew—a useless task it seems,
My hands grown tired, my head weighed down with dreams—
The panoply of war, the martial tread of men,
Grim-faced, stern-eyed, gazing beyond the ken
Of lesser souls, whose eyes have not seen Death
Nor learned to hold their lives but as a breath—
But—I must sit and sew.

I sit and sew—my heart aches with desire—
That pageant terrible, that fiercely pouring fire
On wasted fields, and writhing grotesque things
Once men. My soul in pity flings
Appealing cries, yearning only to go
There in that holocaust of hell, those fields of woe—
But—I must sit and sew.—

The little useless seam, the idle patch;
Why dream I here beneath my homely thatch,
When there they lie in sodden mud and rain,
Pitifully calling me, the quick ones and the slain?
You need, me, Christ! It is no roseate seam
That beckons me—this pretty futile seam,
It stifles me—God, must I sit and sew?

From *Caroling Dusk*, ed. Countée Cullen (1927)

The Proletariat Speaks

ALICE DUNBAR-NELSON

I love beautiful things:
Great trees, bending green winged branches to a velvet lawn,
Fountains sparkling in white marble basins,
Cool fragrance of lilacs and roses and honeysuckle

Or exotic blooms, filling the air with heart-contracting odors;
Spacious rooms, cool and gracious with statues and books,
Carven seats and tapestries, and old masters,
Whose patina shows the wealth of centuries.

And so I work
In a dusty office, whose grimed windows
Look out on an alley of unbelievable squalor,
Where mangy cats, in their degradation, spurn
Swarming bits of meat and bread;
Where odors, vile and breath-taking, rise in fetid waves
Filling my nostrils, scorching my humid, bitter cheeks.

I love beautiful things:
Carven tables laid with lily-hued linen
And fragile china and sparkling iridescent glass;
Pale silver, etched with heraldries,
Where tender bits of regal dainties tempt,
And soft-stepped service anticipates the unspoken wish.

And so I eat
In the food-laden air of a greasy kitchen,
At an oil-clothed table:
Plate piled high with food that turns my head away,
Lest a squeamish stomach reject too soon
The lumpy gobs it never needed.
Or in a smoky cafeteria, balancing a slippery tray
To a table crowded with elbows
Which lately the busboy wiped with a grimy rag.

I love beautiful things:
Soft linen sheets and silken coverlet,
Sweet cool of chamber opened wide to fragrant breeze;
Rose-shaded lamps and golden atomizers,
Spraying Parisian fragrance over my relaxed limbs,
Fresh from a white marble bath, and sweet cool spray.

And so I sleep
In a hot hall-room whose half-opened window,
Unscreened, refuses to budge another inch,
Admits no air, only insects, and hot choking gasps
That make me writhe, nun-like, in sackcloth sheets and lumps
    of straw
And then I rise
To fight my way to a dubious tub,
Whose tiny, tepid stream threatens to make me late;
And hurrying out, dab my unrefreshed face
With bits of toiletry from the ten cent store.

From *The Crisis* (November 1929)

Four Walls

BLANCHE TAYLOR DICKINSON

Four great walls have hemmed me in,
Four strong, high walls:
Right and wrong,
Shall and shan't.

The mighty pillars tremble when
My conscience palls
And sings its song—
I can, I can't.

If for a moment Samson's strength
Were given me I'd shove
Them away from where I stand;
Free, I know I'd love
To ramble soul and all,
And never dread to strike a wall.

Again, I wonder would that be
Such a happy state for me . . .
The going, being, doing, sham—
And never knowing where I am.
I might not love freedom at all;
My tired wings might crave a wall—
Four walls to rise and pen me in
This conscious world with guarded men.

From *Caroling Dusk*, ed. Countée Cullen (1927)

A Dark Actress — Somewhere

BLANCHE TAYLOR DICKINSON

They watched her glide across the stage,
Each one poised with breath a tip-toe,
Felt his soul strings link with hers,
Loosed his heart and let it go
To her brown and tapering fingers,
Crushing it into a ball,
Throwing it with accuracy,
Smiling as she saw it fall.
Bending willow-like to music,
As a bird in willows, singing
Of a love that's so much fancy
From a dream marsh ever springing.
"Art," the critic said next day,
And people flocked to see her play,
Laid their fair hearts at her feet—
But never saw her on the street.

From *The Crisis* (September 1928)

The Palm Wine Seller

GLADYS MAY CASELY HAYFORD

Akosua selling palm wine
In the broiling heat;
Akosua selling palm wine
Down our street

Frothing calabashes
Filled unto the brim,
Boatmen quaffing palm wine
In toil's interim.

Tossing off their palm wine,
Boatmen deem her fair;
Through the haze of palm wine,
Note her jet-black hair.

Roundness of her bosom,
Brilliance of her eyes,
Lips that form a cupid's bow,
Whereon love's dew lies.

Velvet gleam of shoulder,
Arch of bare black feet,
Soft caressing hands,
These her charms complete.

Thus illusioned boatmen
Dwell on 'Kosua's charms,
Blind to fallen bosom,
Knotted thin black arms.

Lips creased in by wrinkles,
Eyes dimmed with the years,
Feet whose arch was altered,
Treading vales of tears.

Hair whose roots life's madness
Knotted and turned wild.
On her heart a load of care,
On her back, a child.

Akosua selling palm wine
In the broiling heat;
Akosua selling palm wine
Down our street.

From *Negro Poets and Their Poems*, ed. Robert T. Kerlin (1923);
Opportunity (February 1930)

The Negro Laughs Back

MARY JENNESS

You laugh, and I must hide the wound
    Your laughter cuts in me;
You strike, and I must turn the cheek
    Like One of Galilee.

And have you never envied me
    The joy that turns your rod, —
You that have made me what I am,
    Condemned to be like God?

From *Opportunity* (August 1928)

Secret

MARY JENNESS

O you that strike will never flinch
    From hearts you cannot feel.
Though I that turn the cheek may hide
    A wound that does not heal.

Yet something in you has to die
    And something in me live—
I thank you for the gift of hate
    That keeps me sensitive!

From *Opportunity* (August 1928)

Epitome

RUTH G. DIXON

(To the lovers of "Porgy," "Scarlet Sister Mary," and other
stories "characteristic" of Negro life.)

Emerges now a hero new,
A soul unknown,
To claim the horizon of your fancy.

Steps out from the dusky veil
A silhouette—black and stark,
Posing in the wake of your applause
All too thunderous.

You fawn, you worship, you adore;
You see a human god and goddess
Hitherto unknown.
They show a new and interesting life—
Souls of lust embroidered to your liking—
Not shaming gazing eyes
But feeding them,
Not piercing human hearts
But salving sores of pride.

You cry "Eureka!" and rejoice.
You've found at last the Negro!
Primitive! Beautiful! Untarnished
By the light of your civilization,
Unfettered by your laws
Of social decency.

O God—forgive the Pharisee—and me—
For I *am* glad that I am not like these
Who see a life "rich and beautiful"
In such utter, helpless degradation.

And yet—to you, my fairer ones,
I am indebted—and somewhat appeased.
I hold not light the tribute you have given,
When in the peons of my race,
When in its outcasts and its prostitutes,
You find not filth
But souls divine and beautiful.

From *The Crisis* (October 1930)

Nordic

LILLIAN BYRNES

He takes his love much as he takes his wine;
He does not sip or taste,
Or gaze upon its long imprisoned sunshine—
He gulps.
Men must perforce get drunk;
It is written somewhere.

And having been drunk,
He curses the wine for being red,
The love for being passion,
Ensnaring him.

Sober and repentant and miserable,
He makes resolutions against wine and love;
So that when he indulges in either,
He can fall—
As people ought who so indulge;
And feel as people ought
About it afterward.

Then he is Puritan.

Or he is lusty, male, resplendent,
Knowing that he should sin
On general principles.
He tosses away the empty glass
Insolently;
Satiate and comfortable,
He consigns the harlot, love,
To her fixed domain of the senses—
Then his is the "Great Blond Beast."

From *The Crisis* (May 1929)

Chalk-Dust

LILLIAN BYRNES

I am tired of chalk-dust.
It drops into the gray wooden trays
Dirtier and grayer for its association with facts;
It floats about the room
Mingled with fine, gray, uninteresting data.
It is made, they say, of countless little creatures
Dead a billion years!
It has the relentless persistence of the long dead.

It gets between me and the rays of sun
That come slanting in at four o'clock
And it hovers in long, perceptible rows
Of particulars of realism.
It makes my hands gritty, and my hair dry;
It sifts into the creases of my garments;
It follows me about;
It permeates my life.

It will strangle me slowly, quietly,
And sift over my body when I, like it,
Am so dead as to be merely useful;
With chalk-like face, chalky garments,
Grit of chalk in my hair—now matching it—
My temper as futilely brittle as chalk;
Chalk in my soul.

I want to roll in wet, green grass,
To plunge headfirst into youth, and music, and laughter;
I am tired, tired, tired—of chalk-dust.

From *The Crisis* (August 1930)

Class Room

VIRGINIA A. HOUSTON

Behind him a picture.
Blue-gray skies,
Phantom clouds
Chasing a topsy-turvy ship
Across an indigo sea . . .

And on those joyous sails
A mirrored image of a bald head,
Shattering my dream
Of faraway, mysterious lands,
Gold-red sunsets,
Silver-white nights,
Of seas shattering against
A sun-splashed deck.

The whisper of the sea in my ears
And the whistle of the wind in the sails
Are replaced by the wheezy murmur
Of an anti-Freudian.

From *The Crisis* (March 1929)

A Brown Aesthete Speaks

MAE V. COWDERY

No: I am neither seeking to change nor keep myself;
Simply acting upon new revelations.

There was a time,
I own,
When I fared, quite pleased with myself,
With my unkempt curls, unhealthy pores—myself;
When Jenny Lind,
In song that brought your tears,
Was like morphine, teasing me to sleep and dream;
When Beecher's cadences stirred no shout in me,
And when I thought it a miracle that
    your visage flushed with delight
    as you recited Aeschylus and Homer.

But since that time, I met Keats and Poe.
(Wisdom can evolve a simple taste,
And love is a feeling deep and universal.)
Now, I perceive:
Ah, you had tasted Beauty!
Now I understand you;
Can interpret you;
Try you by myself,—
Now that Beauty is religion in my soul!
I fired your furnaces,
Served your parties,
Washed your dishes;
Yes, on my knees and hands like a quadruped creature,
I scrubbed your kitchen floor—
That I might learn of Beauty,
Of Keats and Poe.
And why shall I not love Keats and Poe?
Feel their genius,
Marvel at their fire,

Pity their fates,
Laud their martyrdom,
Love the art they loved?
Did I carp when you created beautiful curls,
Becoming curls, to deck your Marcian Bob?
Or of the Bob itself?
Or of how you smiled to hear me sing
Of how Malindy sings?
Or when you required of me the sad songs of my fathers?
Or when your body lilted to the sway of new folk music?
And your nimble feet tangled in the
     double-quick movement of my
     body-wriggling, syncopated dance?
Did I charge that you were aping me?
(Why should I
Or why should anyone?)
I only thought that you were questing Beauty.

Oh friend, let's be kind to one another!
Let us be mutual teachers,
Mutually questing El Dorado;
Lovely Arcady;
Those are wonderful Hands that fashioned us!
Handle those cosmetics softly;
I would more beautify these curls,
This skin,
Would refine this brain.
Oh chide me not if I met Keats and Poe,
If I met Keats and Poe—
And love them!

From *The Crisis* (September 1928)

A Prayer

MAE V. COWDERY

I saw a dark boy
   Trudging on the road
('Twas a dreary road
   Blacker than night).
Oft times he'd stumble
   And stagger 'neath his burden
But still he kept trudging
   Along that dreary road.

I heard a dark boy
   Singing as he passed;
Oft times he'd laugh
   But still a tear
Crept thru his song,
   As he kept trudging
Along that weary road.

I saw a long white mist roll down
   And cover all the earth
(There wasn't even a shadow
   To tell it was night.)
And then there came an echo . . .
   . . . Footsteps of a dark boy
Still climbing on the way.

A song with its tear
   And then a prayer
From the lips of a dark boy
   Struggling thru the fog.
Oft times I'd hear

   The lashing of a whip
And then a voice would cry to heaven:
   "Lord! . . . Lord!

Have mercy . . . mercy!"
And still that bleeding body
    Pushed onward thru the fog.
Songs . . . Tears . . . Blood . . . Prayer
    Throbbing thru the mist.

The mist rolled by
    And the sun shone fair,
Fair and golden,
    On a dark boy . . . cold and still
High on a bare bleak tree
    His face upturned to heaven,
His soul upraised in song,
    "Peace . . . Peace
    Rest in the Lord."

Oft times in the twilight
    I can hear him still singing
As he walks in the heavens,
    A song without a tear,
A prayer without a plea . . .

Lord, lift me up to the purple sky
    That lays its hand of stars
Tenderly on my bowed head
    As I kneel high on this barren hill.
My song holds naught but tears,
    My prayer is but a plea.
Lord take me to the clouds
    To sleep . . . to sleep.

From *The Crisis* (September 1928)

The Lynching

DOROTHEA MATHEWS

He saw the rope, the moving mob,
And suddenly thought of quiet things;
The way the river-ripples sob,
The silver flight of pigeon's wings
Free in the blue September air;
And that the night was warm and brown—
Under the trees the shadows hung;
The little stars of God looked down.

From *Opportunity* (April 1928)

The Road

HELENE JOHNSON

Ah, little road, all whirry in the breeze,
A leaping clay hill lost among the trees,
The bleeding note of rapture-streaming thrush
Caught in a drowsy hush
And stretched out in a single, singing line of dusky song.
Ah, little road, brown as my race is brown,
Your trodden beauty like our trodden pride,
Dust of the dust, they must not bruise you down.
Rise to one brimming golden, spilling cry!

From *Opportunity* (July 1926); *The Book of American Negro Poetry*,
ed. James Weldon Johnson (1931)

TWO

Heritage

Bottled

HELENE JOHNSON

Upstairs on the third floor
Of the 135th Street library
In Harlem, I saw a little
Bottle of sand, brown sand,
Just like the kids make pies
Out of down at the beach.
But the label said: "This
Sand was taken from the Sahara desert."
Imagine that! The Sahara desert!
Some bozo's been all the way to Africa to get some sand.

And yesterday on Seventh Avenue
I saw a darky dressed to kill
In yellow gloves and swallowtail coat
And swirling a cane. And everyone
Was laughing at him. Me too,
At first, till I saw his face
When he stopped to hear a
Organ grinder grind out some jazz.
Boy! You should a seen that darky's face!
It just shone. Gee, he was happy!
And he began to dance. No
Charleston or Black Bottom for him.
No sir. He danced just as dignified
And slow. No, not slow either.
Dignified and *proud*! You couldn't
Call it slow, not with all the
Cuttin' up he did. You would a died to see him.

The crowd kept yellin' but he didn't hear,
Just kept on dancin' and twirlin' that cane
And yellin' out loud every once in a while.
I know the crowd thought he was coo-coo.
But say, I was where I could see his face,

And somehow, I could see him dancin' in a jungle,
A real honest-to-cripe jungle, and he wouldn't leave on them
Trick clothes—those yaller shoes and yaller gloves
And swallowtail coat. He wouldn't have on nothing.
And he wouldn't be carrying no cane.
He'd be carrying a spear with a sharp fine point
Like the bayonets we had "over there."
And the end of it would be dipped in some kind of
Hoo-doo poison. And he'd be dancin' black and naked and
    gleaming.
And he'd have rings in his ears and on his nose
And bracelets and necklaces of elephants' teeth.
Gee, I bet he'd be beautiful then all right.
No one would laugh at him then, I bet.
Say! That man that took that sand from the Sahara desert
And put it in a little bottle on a shelf in the library,
That's what they done to this shine, ain't it? Bottled him.
Trick shoes, trick coat, trick cane, trick everything—all glass—
But inside—
Gee, that poor shine!

From *Negro Poets and Their Poems*, ed. Robert T. Kerlin (1923);
Caroling Dusk, ed. Countée Cullen (1927)

Sonnet to a Negro in Harlem

HELENE JOHNSON

You are disdainful and magnificent—
Your perfect body and your pompous gait,
Your dark eyes flashing solemnly with hate;
Small wonder that you are incompetent
To imitate those whom you so despise—
Your shoulders towering high above the throng,
Your head thrown back in rich, barbaric song,
Palm trees and mangoes stretched before your eyes.
Let others toil and sweat for labor's sake
And wring from grasping hands their meed of gold.
Why urge ahead your supercilious feet?
Scorn will efface each footprint that you make.
I love your laughter, arrogant and bold.
You are too splendid for this city street!

From *Negro Poets and Their Poems*, ed. Robert T. Kerlin (1923);
Caroling Dusk, ed. Countée Cullen (1927); *The Book of American
Negro Poetry*, ed. James Weldon Johnson (1931)

Poem

HELENE JOHNSON

Little brown boy,
Slim, dark, big-eyed,
Crooning love songs to your banjo
Down at the Lafayette—
Gee, boy, I love the way you hold your head,
High sort of and a bit to one side,
Like a prince, a jazz prince. And I love
Your eyes flashing, and your hands,
And your patent-leathered feet,
And your shoulders jerking the jig-wa.
And I love your teeth flashing,
And the way your hair shines in the spotlight
Like it was the real stuff.
Gee, brown boy, I loves you all over.
I'm glad I'm a jig. I'm glad I can
Understand your dancin' and your
Singin', and feel all the happiness
And joy and don't care in you.
Gee, boy, when you sing, I can close my ears
And hear tom-toms just as plain.
Listen to me, will you, what do I know
About tom-toms? But I like the word, sort of,
Don't you? It belongs to us.
Gee, boy, I love the way you hold your head,
And the way you sing, and dance,
And everything.
Say, I think you're wonderful. You're
Allright with me,
You are.

From *Caroling Dusk*, ed. Countée Cullen (1927); *The Book of American Negro Poetry*, ed. James Weldon Johnson (1931)

Magalu

HELENE JOHNSON

Summer comes.
The ziczac hovers
'Round the greedy-mouthed crocodile.
A vulture bears away a foolish jackal.
The flamingo is a dash of pink
Against dark green mangroves,
Her slender legs rivalling her slim neck.
The laughing lake gurgles delicious music in its throat
And lulls to sleep the lazy lizard,
A nebulous being on a sun-scorched rock.
In such a place,
In this pulsing, riotous gasp of color,
I met Magalu, dark as a tree at night,
Eager-lipped, listening to a man with a white collar
And a small black book with a cross on it.
Oh Magalu, come! Take my hand and I will read you poetry,
Chromatic words,
Seraphic symphonies,
Fill up your throat with laughter and your heart with song.
Do not let him lure you from your laughing waters,
Lulling lakes, lissome winds.
Would you sell the colors of your sunset and the fragrance
Of your flowers, and the passionate wonder of your forest
For a creed that will not let you dance?

From *Caroling Dusk*, ed. Countée Cullen (1927)

My Race

HELENE JOHNSON

Ah, my race,
Hungry race,
Throbbing and young—
Ah, my race,
Wonder race,
Sobbing with song—
Ah, my race,
Laughing race,
Careless in mirth—
Ah, my veiled
Unformed race,
Fumbling in birth.

From *Opportunity* (July 1925)

Heritage

GWENDOLYN B. BENNETT

I want to see the slim palm-trees,
Pulling at the clouds
With little pointed fingers. . . .

I want to see lithe Negro girls
Etched dark against the sky
While sunset lingers.

I want to hear the silent sands,
Singing to the moon
Before the Sphinx-still face. . . .

I want to hear the chanting
Around a heathen fire
Of a strange black race.

I want to breathe the Lotus flow'r,
Sighing to the stars
With tendrils drinking at the Nile. . . .

I want to feel the surging
Of my sad people's soul,
Hidden by a minstrel-smile.

From *Opportunity* (December 1923); *The Book of American
Negro Poetry*, ed. James Weldon Johnson (1931)

To Usward

GWENDOLYN B. BENNETT

Dedicated to all Negro Youth known and unknown who
have a song to sing, a story to tell or a vision for the sons of
earth. Especially dedicated to Jessie Fauset upon the event of
her novel, *There Is Confusion.*

Let us be still
As ginger jars are still
Upon a Chinese shelf.
And let us be contained
By entities of Self. . . .
Not still with lethargy and sloth,
But quiet with the pushing of our growth.
Not self-contained with smug identity
But conscious of the strength in entity.
If any have a song to sing
That's different from the rest,
Oh let them sing
Before the urgency of Youth's behest!
For some of us have songs to sing
Of jungle heat and fires,
And some of us are solemn grown
With pitiful desires,
And there are those who feel the pull
Of seas beneath the skies,
And some there be who want to croon
Of Negro lullabies.
We claim no part with racial dearth;
We want to sing the songs of birth!
And so we stand like ginger jars
Like ginger jars bound 'round
With dust and age;
Like jars of ginger we are sealed

By nature's heritage.
But let us break the seal of years
With pungent thrusts of song,
For there is joy in long-dried tears
For whetted passions of a throng!

From *The Crisis* (May 1924)

Song

GWENDOLYN B. BENNETT

I am weaving a song of waters,
Shaken from firm, brown limbs,
Or heads thrown back in irreverent mirth.
My song has the lush sweetness
Of moist, dark lips
Where hymns keep company
With old forgotten banjo songs.
Abandon tells you
That I sing the heart of a race
While sadness whispers
That I am the cry of a soul. . . .

A-shoutin' in de ole camp-meetin-place,
A-strummin' o' de ole banjo.
Singin' in de moonlight,
Sobbin' in de dark.
Singin', sobbin', strummin' slow . . .
Singin' slow, sobbin' low.
Strummin', strummin', strummin' slow . . .
Words are bright bugles
That make the shining for my song,
And mothers hold brown babes
To dark, warm breasts
To make my singing sad.

A dancing girl with swaying hips
Sets mad the queen in a harlot's eye.
   Praying slave
   Jazz-band after
   Breaking heart
   To the time of laughter . . .
Clinking chains and minstrelsy
Are welded fast with melody.
   A praying slave

With a jazz-band after . . .
Singin' slow, sobbin' low.
Sun-baked lips will kiss the earth.
Throats of bronze will burst with mirth.
Sing a little faster,
Sing a little faster,
Sing!

From *The New Negro*, ed. Alain Locke (1925); *Opportunity*
(October 1926)

To a Dark Girl

GWENDOLYN B. BENNETT

I love you for your brownness
And the rounded darkness of your breast.
I love you for the breaking sadness in your voice
And shadows where your wayward eye-lids rest.

Something of old forgotten queens
Lurks in the lithe abandon of your walk
And something of the shackled slave
Sobs in the rhythm of your talk.

Oh, little brown girl, born for sorrow's mate,
Keep all you have of queenliness,
Forgetting that you once were slave,
And let your full lips laugh at Fate!

From *Negro Poets and Their Poems*, ed. Robert T. Kerlin (1923);
Opportunity (October 1927); *Anthology of American Negro
Literature*, ed. V. J. Calverton (1929); *The Book of American
Negro Poetry*, ed. James Weldon Johnson (1931)

The Shining Parlor

ANITA SCOTT COLEMAN

It was a drab street
A white man's street . . .
Jammed with automobiles
Streetcars and trucks;
   Bee-hived with fruit vendors' stalls,
   Real estate concerns, meat shops,
Dental clinics, and soft drink stands.

It was a drab street
A white man's street . . .
But it held the shining parlor—
A boot-black booth,
   Commandeered by a black man,
   Who spent much time smiling out
Upon the hub-bub of the thoroughfare.

Ever . . . serenely smiling . . .
With a brush and a soiled rag in his hands.
Often . . . white patrons wait for
Their boots to be "shined,"
   Wondering the while
   At the wonder—
Of the black man's smile.

From *The Crisis* (September 1929)

Black Faces

ANITA SCOTT COLEMAN

I love black faces. . . .
They are full of smould'ring fire.
And Negro eyes, white—with white desire,
And Negro lips so soft and thick,
Like rich velvet within
Fine jewelry cases.
I love black faces. . . .

From *Opportunity* (October 1929)

Negro Laughter

ANITA SCOTT COLEMAN

Negro laughter . . .
  is not the laughter of those others
Who force their distrait mirth
  through thin pale lips.

Negro laughter . . .
  is a stem of joyousness, a hardy tendril
Thrusting through the moraines
  of long distress.

From *The Crisis* (March 1930)

Black Baby

ANITA SCOTT COLEMAN

The baby I hold in my arms is a black baby.
  Today I set him in the sun and
  Sunbeams danced on his head.
The baby I hold in my arms is a black baby.
  I toil, and I cannot always cuddle him.
  I place him on the ground at my feet.
  He presses the warm earth with his hands,
  He lifts the sand and laughs to see
  It flow through his chubby fingers.
  I watch to discern which are his hands,
  Which is the sand. . . .
Lo . . . the rich loam is black like his hands.

The baby I hold in my arms is a black baby.
  Today the coal-man brought me coal.
  Sixteen dollars a ton is the price I pay for coal.—
  Costly fuel . . . though they say:—
  Men must sweat and toil to dig it from the ground.
  Costly fuel . . . 'Tis said:—
  If it is buried deep enough and lies hidden long enough
  'Twill be no longer coal but diamonds. . . .
  My black baby looks at me.
  His eyes are like coals,
  They shine like diamonds.

From *Opportunity* (February 1929)

Baby Cobina

GLADYS MAY CASELY HAYFORD

Brown Baby Cobina, with his large black velvet eyes,
His little coos of ecstacies, his gurgling of surprise,
With brass bells on his ankles, that laugh where'er he goes;
It's so rare for bells to tinkle, above brown dimpled toes.

Brown Baby Cobina is so precious that we fear
Something might come and steal him, when we grownups are
  not near;
So we tied bells on his ankles, and kissed on them this charm—
"Bell, guard our Baby Cobina from all devils and all harm."

From *Caroling Dusk*, ed. Countée Cullen (1927)

Lullaby

Close your sleepy eyes, or the pale moonlight will steal you,
Else in the mystic silence, the moon will turn you white.
Then you won't see the sunshine, nor smell the open roses,
Nor love your Mammy anymore, whose skin is dark as night.
You will only love the shadows, and the foam upon the billows,
The shadow of the vulture's wings, the call of mystery,
The hooting of the night owl, and the howling of the jackal,
The sighing of the evil winds, the call of mystery.
Wherever moonlight stretches her arms across the heavens,
You will follow, always follow, till you become instead,
A shade in human draperies, with palm fronds for your pillow,
In place of Mammy's bibini,* asleep on his wee bed.

From *The Crisis* (March 1929)

* "Bibini" is Fanti for baby boy.

Rime for the Christmas Baby
(At 48 Webster Place, Orange)

ANNE SPENCER

Dear Bess,
    He'll have rings and linen things,
    And others made of silk;
    There'll be toys like other boys'
    And cream upon his milk;
    True, some sort of merit in a mart
    Where goods are sold for money,
    But packed with comfort is the heart
    That shares with you what's funny;
    So, please, kiss him when he's very bad
    And laugh with him in gladness,—
    Life is too long a way to go,
    And age will bring him sadness . . .
    Pray you for unceasing springs,
    Swelling deep in pard'n,
    That into twin lives may grow
    Time's unfading garden.

From *Opportunity* (December 1927)

Grapes: Still-Life

ANNE SPENCER

Snugly you rest, sweet globes,
Aged essence of the sun;
Copper of the platter
Like that you lie upon.

Is so well your heritage
You need feel no change
From the ringlet of your stem
To this bright rim's flange;

You, green-white Niagara,
Cool dull Nordic of your kind,—
Does your thick meat flinch
From these . . . touch and press your rind?

Caco, there, so close to you,
Is the beauty of the vine;
Stamen red and pistil black
Thru the curving line;

Concord, the too peaceful one,
Purpling at your side,
All the colors of his flask
Holding high in pride . . .

This, too, is your heritage,
You who force the plight;
Blood and bone you turn to them
For their root is white.

From *The Crisis* (April 1929)

The Bronze Legacy
(To a Brown Boy)

EFFIE LEE NEWSOME

'Tis a noble gift to be brown, all brown,
    Like the strongest things that make up this earth,
Like the mountains grave and grand,
    Even like the trunks of trees—
    Even oaks, to be like those!
God builds His strength in bronze.

To be brown like thrush and lark!
    Like the subtle wren so dark!
Nay, the king of beasts wears brown;
    Eagles are of this same hue.
I thank God, then, I am brown.
    Brown has mighty things to do.

From *The Crisis* (October 1922)

Morning Light
(The Dew-Drier)

EFFIE LEE NEWSOME

Brother to the firefly—
For as the firefly lights the night,
So lights he the morning—
Bathed in the dank dews as he goes forth
Through heavy menace and mystery
Of half-waking tropic dawn;
Behold a little black boy,
A naked black boy,
Sweeping aside with his slight frame
Night's pregnant tears,
And making a morning path to the light
For the tropic traveler!

Bathed in the blood of battle,
Treading toward a new morning,
May not his race, its body long bared
To the world's disdain, its face schooled to smile
For a light to come;
May not his race, even as the dew-boy leads,
Light onward men's minds toward a time
When tolerance, forbearance,
Such as reigned in the heart of One
Whose heart was gold,
Shall shape the earth for that fresh dawning
After the dews of blood?

From *Caroling Dusk*, ed. Countée Cullen (1927)

Heritage

MAE V. COWDERY

It is a blessed heritage
To wear pain,
A bright smile on our lips.
Our dark fathers gave us
The gift of shedding sorrow
In a song.

From *We Lift Our Voices* (1936)

Beauty

OCTAVIA BEATRICE WYNBUSH

'Tis wondrous strange in what things men find beauty.
One sees it in the sun kissing the sleeping hills awake;
Another in the moon, trailing paths to fairy-land across the
    slow-moving water.
This man finds beauty in first youth; his friend, in mature
    woman.
But beauty lurks for me in black, knotted hands,
Hands consecrated to toil that those who come
Behind them may have tender, shapely hands;
And beautiful are shoulders with bearing heavy burdens stooped
That younger shoulders may grow straight and proud.
And faces, dark, sad faces, too, are beautiful—
The patient, wistful faces of the many
Who have viewed their lands of promise from afar,
Turned from the mountain to the lonely path
Of sober duty, and gazed on
The promised land no more.
'Tis wondrous strange
In what things men find beauty.

From *Opportunity* (August 1930)

The True American

GEORGIA DOUGLAS JOHNSON

America, here is your son, born of your iron heel;
Black blood and red and white contend along this frame of
    steel.
The thorns deep in his brow are set and yet he does not cower;
He goes with neither fears nor tears to crucifixion hour.
Nor yet does hatred blur his view of mankind's frail parade;
From his commanding triple coign, all prejudices fade.
The ebbing nations coalesce in him and flow as one;
The bright shining rainbow sweeping back to God at set of sun!
Mark well the surety of tread, the new song high in air,
The new note in the nation's throat, as permanent as prayer.
America, regard your son, The Cosmopolitan,
The pattern of posterity, The True American.

From *The Crisis* (April 1927)

Oriflamme

JESSIE FAUSET

I can remember when I was a little, young girl, how my old mammy would sit out of doors in the evenings and look up at the stars and groan, and I would say, "Mammy, what makes you groan so?" And she would say, "I am groaning to think of my poor children; they do not know where I be and I don't know where they be. I look up at the stars and they look up at the stars!"

—Sojourner Truth

I think I see her sitting, bowed and black,
    Stricken and seared with slavery's mortal scars,
Reft of her children, lonely, anguished, yet
    Still looking at the stars.

Symbolic mother, we thy myriad sons,
    Pounding our stubborn hearts on Freedom's bars,
Clutching our birthright, fight with faces set,
    Still visioning the stars!

From *The Crisis* (January 1920); *Negro Poets and Their Poems*, ed. Robert T. Kerlin (1923); *The Book of American Negro Poetry*, ed. James Weldon Johnson (1931).

To Keep the Memory of Charlotte Forten Grimké — 1915

ANGELINA WELD GRIMKÉ

Still are there wonders of the dark and day;
The muted shrilling of shy things at night,
So small beneath the stars and moon;
The peace, dream-frail, but perfect while the light
Lies softly on the leaves at noon.
These are, and these will be
   Until eternity;
But she who loved them well has gone away.

Each dawn, while yet the east is veil'd grey,
The birds about her window wake and sing;
And far away, each day, some lark
I know is singing where the grasses swing;
Some robin calls and calls at dark.
These are, and these will be
   Until eternity;
But she who loved them well has gone away.

The wild flowers that she loved down green ways stray;
Her roses lift their wistful buds at dawn,
But not for eyes that loved them best;
Only her little pansies are all gone,
Some lying softly on her breast.
And flowers will bud and be
   Until eternity;
But she who loved them well has gone away.

Where has she gone? And who is there to say?
But this we know: her gentle spirit moves
And is where beauty never wanes,
Perchance by other streams, 'mid other groves:

And to us here, ah! she remains
A lovely memory
    Until eternity;
She came, she loved, and then she went away.

Negro Poets and Their Poems, ed. Robert T. Kerlin (1923); *The Crisis* (November 1931)

An Old Slave Woman

JOYCE SIMS CARRINGTON

She
Is like
A wrinkled apple,
Old and brown,
Clinging
By its fragile stem
To life.

You
Cannot say
That hers
Were
Empty hands;
For
About her sons
Is wound
The golden thread
Of Hope and Love,
And
In their faces
Shines
The rising sun.

From *Opportunity* (March 1926)

THREE

~~~~~~~~~~~~~~~~~~

Love and Passion

Longings

MAE V. COWDERY

To dance—
In the light of moon,
A platinum moon,
Poised like a slender dagger
On the velvet darkness of night.

To dream—
'Neath the bamboo trees
On the sable breast
Of earth—
And listen to the wind.

To croon—
Weird sweet melodies
Round the cabin door
With banjos clinking softly—
And from out the shadow
Hear the beat of tom-toms
Resonant through the years.

To plunge—
My brown body
In a golden pool,
And lazily float on the swell,
Watching the rising sun.

To stand—
On a purple mountain
Hidden from earth
By mists of dreams
And tears—

To talk—
With God.

From *The Crisis* (December 1927)

Exultation

MAE V. COWDERY

O day!
With sun glowing—
Gold
Pouring through
A scarlet rustling tree!

O night!
With stars burning—
Fire falling
Into a dark and whispering sea!

From *We Lift Our Voices* (1936)

Insatiate

MAE V. COWDERY

If my love were meat and bread
And sweet cool wine to drink,
They would not be enough,
For I must have a finer table spread
To sate my entity.

If her lips were rubies red,
Her eyes two sapphires blue,
Her fingers ten sticks of white jade,
Coral tipped . . . and her hair of purple hue
Hung down in a silken shawl . . .
They would not be enough
To fill the coffers of my need.

If her thoughts were arrows
Ever speeding true
Into the core of my mind,
And her voice round notes of melody
No nightingale or lark
Could ever hope to sing . . .
Not even these would be enough
To keep my constancy.

But if my love did whisper
Her song into another's ear
Or place the tip of one pink nail
Upon another's hand,
Then would I forever be
A willing prisoner . . .
Chained to her side by uncertainty!

From *We Lift Our Voices* (1936)

Farewell

MAE V. COWDERY

No more
The feel of your hand
On my breast
Like the silver path
Of the moon
On dark heaving ocean.

No more
The rumpled softness
Of your hair
Like wind
In leafy shadowed trees.

No more
The lush sweetness
Of your lips
Like dew
On new-opened moonflowers.

No more
The drowsy murmurings
Of your voice
Like the faint twitter
Of birds before dawn.

No more
The poignant melody
Of hours spent
Between moonlight
And sunrise
Like the song
Of a crystal river
Going out to sea . . .

Only the awful sound
Of silence
In that hour
Before dawn
When the moon has waned,
The stars died,
And the sun is buried in mist.

From *The Crisis* (February 1929)

Having Had You

MAE V. COWDERY

Having had you once
And lost you,
It is too much to ask
For you again.

Having heard your voice,
The words of other lovers
Are stones . . . falling into an empty well.

Having known your kiss,
The lips of other lovers
Are withered leaves . . . upon the wind.

Were you a God
I could build a shrine
And worship you.

Ah . . . if you were but the moon,
I could snare you
In the branches of a tree!

Were you anything
But what you are . . .
A dream come true
And now a dream again . . .
I might have you back!

But having had you once
And lost you,
It is too much
To want you back again!

From *The Crisis* (August 1930)

Some Hands Are Lovelier

MAE V. COWDERY

Two trees breathe
The same sweet air,
And sun, and rain—
And whisper
To the moonless night
The same dim prayer
Of star-wrought wonder.

Two trees stand
Above a red, red road
Whose branches touch
And now withdraw . . . and meet again
In undreamed ecstasy.

Some lips are sweeter
To capture in mad beauty
And then release—
Some hands are lovelier
To clasp awhile—
And then let go!

From *We Lift Our Voices* (1936)

Poem . . . for a Lover

MAE V. COWDERY

I would give you
The blue-violet dreams
Of clouds . . . forgotten
And left to grow old
In the sky.

I would give you
The dew-drenched hope
Of flowers . . . forgotten
By a long dead lover
And left in a garden to die.

But you have no need
Of my meagre gifts
With your gay little songs
And lips . . . redder
Than bitter-sweet berries
Left on a leafless bush
By the frost . . .

From *We Lift Our Voices* (1936)

If I Must Know

MAE V. COWDERY

If I must know sorrow
To live
Then burden my soul
With the frustrated dreams
Of good women!

If I must know torture
Then bind me with vows
To complacency!

If I must know love
To live
Then be quick!
Give me back this elusive thing
Men call love!

From *The Crisis* (July 1930)

Lines to a Sophisticate

MAE V. COWDERY

Never would I seek
To capture you with tempestuous ardor
Nor hold you at arm's length
In carnal anticipation. . . .
But like a wine of rare vintage
I would savor and sip slowly
That I might know each separate scent
Of your elusive fragrance.

Never would I seek to capture all your beauty
And imprison it in the mouldy bottle of my lust;
Rather would I pour it into the chalice of my love
And let its bouquet escape to mingle with the air
That I might breathe again your perfume
Long after you are gone. . . .

From *We Lift Our Voices* (1936)

Dusk

MAE V. COWDERY

Like you
Letting down your
Purple-shadowed hair
To hide the rose and gold
Of your loveliness
And your eyes peeping thru
Like beacon lights
In the gathering darkness.

From *Ebony and Topaz*, ed. Charles S. Johnson (1927)

To a Dark Dancer

MARJORIE MARSHALL

Within the shadow of the moon you danced
Or postured in the light of crystal stars,
Your dark flame-beauty challenging a glance;
You flung a sob-caught laugh and leaped afar
Into the arms of night, with upturned face
That mocked the waning beauty of the moon,
Its fragile curves, which lacked your Nile-born grace,
Which made the tom-toms beat, the senses swoon.

You dance no more upon the silvered sand
With streaming midnight hair and panting breath,
But lie in peace while gold and jeweled bands
Adorn your wrists, and silks caress your breast;
For you are dead and even as I wait
The desert moon has veiled its pale-gold face.

From *The Crisis* (January 1928)

Night's Protégé

MARJORIE MARSHALL

Child of bewitching night—
    Ah, but she is exquisite!
Her soft gold-amber fingers
    Curl back like tender petals
And, clinging softly, linger
    Lightly on her pulsing lips.

Lass of enchanting light—
    Ah, but she is exquisite!
Her eyes of melted night
    Mirror the star-gleam lurking
In curls of dark delight,
    Throbbing with an angel's kiss.

From *The Crisis* (July 1931)

Joy

CLARISSA SCOTT DELANY

Joy shakes me like the wind that lifts a sail,
Like the roistering wind
That laughs through stalwart pines.
It floods me like the sun
On rain-drenched trees
That flash with silver and green.

I abandon myself to joy—
I laugh—I sing.
Too long have I walked a desolate way,
Too long stumbled down a maze
Bewildered.

From *Opportunity* (October 1926)

Interim

CLARISSA SCOTT DELANY

The night was made for rest and sleep,
For winds that softly sigh;
It was not made for grief and tears;
So then why do I cry?

The wind that blows through leafy trees
Is soft and warm and sweet;
For me the night is a gracious cloak
To hide my soul's defeat.

Just one dark hour of shaken depths,
Of bitter black despair—
Another day will find me brave,
And not afraid to dare.

From *Negro Poets and Their Poems*, ed. Robert T. Kerlin (1923)

The Mask

CLARISSA SCOTT DELANY

So detached and cool she is,
No motion e'er betrays
The secret life within her soul,
The anguish of her days.

She seems to look upon the world
With cold ironic eyes,
To spurn emotion's fevered sway,
To scoff at tears and sighs.

But once a woman with a child
Passed by her on the street,
And once she heard from casual lips
A man's name, bitter-sweet.

Such baffled yearning in her eyes,
Such pain upon her face!
I turned aside until the mask
Was slipped once more in place.

From *Negro Poets and Their Poems*, ed. Robert T. Kerlin (1923);
Caroling Dusk, ed. Countée Cullen (1927)

To Clarissa Scott Delany

ANGELINA WELD GRIMKÉ

She has not found herself a hard pillow
   And a long hard bed,

A chilling cypress, a wan willow
   For her gay young head . . .
   These are for the dead.

Does the violet-lidded twilight die
   And the piercing dawn
And the white clear moon and the night-blue sky . . .

Does the shimmering note
In the shy, shy throat
Of the swaying bird?

O, does children's laughter
Live not after
It is heard?

Does the dear, dear shine upon dear, dear things,
In the eyes, on the hair,
On waters, on wings . . .
Live no more anywhere?

Does the tang of the sea, the breath of frail flowers,
   Of fern crushed, of clover,
Of grasses at dark, of the earth after showers
   Not linger, not hover?

Does the beryl in tarns, the soft orchid in haze,
The primrose through treetops, the unclouded jade
Of the north sky, all earth's flamings and russets and grays
   Simply smudge out and fade?

And all loveliness, all sweetness, all grace,
All the gay questing, all wonder, all dreaming,
They that cup beauty, that veiled opaled vase,
Are they only the soul of seeming?

O, hasn't she found just a little, thin door
And passed through and closed it between?
O, aren't those her light feet upon that light floor,
. . . That her laughter? . . . O, doesn't she lean
As we do to listen? . . . O, doesn't it mean
    She is only unseen, unseen?

From *American Negro Poetry*, ed. Arna Bontemps (1963)

A Mona Lisa

ANGELINA WELD GRIMKÉ

1.

I should like to creep
Through the long brown grasses
   That are your lashes;
I should like to poise
   On the very brink
Of the leaf-brown pools
   That are your shadowed eyes;
I should like to cleave
   Without sound,
Their glimmering waters,
   Their unrippled waters;
I should like to sink down
   And down
      And down . . .
         And deeply drown.

2.

Would I be more than a bubble breaking?
   Or an ever-widening circle
   Ceasing at the marge?
Would my white bones
   Be the only white bones
Wavering back and forth, back and forth
   In their depths?

From *Caroling Dusk*, ed. Countée Cullen (1927)

I Weep

ANGELINA WELD GRIMKÉ

—I weep—
Not as the young do noisily,
Not as the aged rustily,
But quietly.
Drop by drop, the great tears
Splash upon my hands,
And save you saw them shine,
You would not know
I wept.

From *Caroling Dusk*, ed. Countée Cullen (1927)

El Beso

ANGELINA WELD GRIMKÉ

Twilight—and you
Quiet—the stars;
Snare of the shine of your teeth,
Your provocative laughter,
The gloom of your hair;
Lure of you, eye and lip;
Yearning, yearning,
Languor, surrender;
   Your mouth,
And madness, madness,
Tremulous, breathless, flaming,
The space of a sigh;
Then awakening—remembrance,
Pain, regret—your sobbing;
And again, quiet—the stars,
Twilight—and you.

From *Negro Poets and Their Poems*, ed. Robert T. Kerlin (1923)

The Want of You

ANGELINA WELD GRIMKÉ

A hint of gold where the moon will be;
Through the flocking clouds just a star or two;
Leaf sounds, soft and wet and hushed;
And oh! the crying want of you.

From *Negro Poets and Their Poems*, ed. Robert T. Kerlin (1923)

Rainy Season Love Song

GLADYS MAY CASELY HAYFORD

Out of the tense awed darkness, my Frangepani comes:
Whilst the blades of Heaven flash round her, and the roll of
     thunder drums,
My young heart leaps and dances, with exquisite joy and pain,
As, storms within and storms without, I meet my love in the
     rain.

"The rain is in love with you darling; it's kissing you
     everywhere,
Rain pattering over your small brown feet, rain in your curly
     hair;
Rain in the vale that your twin breasts make, as in delicate
     mounds they rise;
I hope there is rain in your heart, Frangepani, as rain half fills
     your eyes."

Into my hands she cometh, and the lightning of my desire
Flashes and leaps about her, more subtle than Heaven's fire;
"The lightning's in love with you darling; it is loving you so
     much
That its warm electricity in you pulses wherever I may touch.
When I kiss your lips and your eyes, and your hands like twin
     flowers apart,
I know there is lightning, Frangepani, deep in the depths of your
     heart."

The thunder rumbles about us, and I feel its triumphant note
As your warm arms steal around me, and I kiss your dusky
     throat;
"The thunder's in love with you darling; it hides its power in
     your breast,
And I feel it stealing o'er me as I lie in your arms at rest.
I sometimes wonder, beloved, when I drink from life's proffered
     bowl,

Whether there's thunder hidden in the innermost parts of your
   soul."

Out of my arms she stealeth, and I am left alone with the night,
Void of all sounds save peace, the first faint glimmer of light.
Into some quiet, hushed stillness my Frangepani goes.
Is there peace within the peace without? Only the darkness
   knows.

From *Caroling Dusk*, ed. Countée Cullen (1927)

The Serving Girl

GLADYS MAY CASELY HAYFORD

The calabash wherein she served my food
Was smooth and polished as sandalwood;
Fish, as white as the foam of the sea,
Peppered, and golden fried for me.
She brought palm wine that carelessly slips
From the sleeping palm tree's honeyed lips.
But who can guess, or even surmise,
The countless things she served with her eyes?

From *Caroling Dusk*, ed. Countée Cullen (1927)

To E.J.J.

ETHEL M. CAUTION

Sparkling eyes of diamond jet;
Wilful hair a-curling yet;
Rounded cheeks and lips well set—
Lips a-smiling, smiling yet;
Slender fingers quick to do
Gracious things for me and you;
Feet that never weary grow
Lightening of another's woe;
Heart a-bubbling o'er with love
From the Fountain-head above;
Life all laughter, words of cheer
Echoing down and down the year;
Loved her well when first we met,
And I love her, love her yet.

From *The Crisis* (August 1930)

Last Night

ETHEL M. CAUTION

Last night I danced on the rim of the moon,
  Delirious and gay,
Quite different from the mood
  I wear about by day.

Athwart my vibrant body
  A chiffon cloud I flung,
Diaphanous and azure,
  With starpoint brilliants hung.

And oh! my feet flew madly!
  My body whirled and swayed!
My soul danced in its ecstasy,
  Untrammeled, unafraid!

Last night I danced on the rim of the moon,
  Delirious and gay,
Then slipped into my sober self
  Just ere the break of day.

From *The Crisis* (February 1929)

Stars in Alabama

JESSIE FAUSET

In Alabama
Stars hang down so low,
So low, they purge the soul
With their infinity.
Beneath their holy glance
Essential good
Rises to mingle with them
In that skiey sea.

At noon
Within the sandy cotton-field
Beyond the clay, red road
Bordered with green,
A Negro lad and lass
Cling hand in hand,
And passion, hot-eyed, hot-lipped,
Lurks unseen.

But in the evening
When the skies lean down,
He's but a wistful boy,
A saintly maiden she,
For Alabama stars
Hang down so low,
So low, they purge the soul
With their infinity.

From *The Crisis* (January 1928)

Fragment

JESSIE FAUSET

The breath of life imbued those few dim days!
Yet all we had was this,—
A flashing smile, a touch of hands, and once
A fleeting kiss.

Blank futile death inheres these years between!
Still, naught have you and I
But frozen tears, and stifled words, and once
A sharp caught cry!

From *Caroling Dusk*, ed. Countée Cullen (1927)

Touché

JESSIE FAUSET

Dear, when we sit in that high, placid room,
"Loving" and "doving" as all lovers do,
Laughing and leaning so close in the gloom,—

What is the change that creeps sharp over you?
Just as you raise your fine hand to my hair,
Bringing that glance of mixed wonder and rue?

"Black hair," you murmur, "so lustrous and rare,
Beautiful too, like a raven's smooth wing;
Surely no gold locks were ever more fair."

Why do you say every night that same thing?
Turning your mind to some old constant theme,
Half meditating and half murmuring?

Tell me, that girl of your young manhood's dream,
Her you loved first in that dim long ago—
Had *she* blue eyes? Did *her* hair goldly gleam?

Does *she* come back to you softly and slow,
Stepping wraith-wise from the depths of the past?
Quickened and fired by the warmth of our glow?

There, I've divined it! My wit holds you fast.
Nay, no excuses; 'tis little I care.
I knew a lad in my own girlhood's past,—
Blue eyes he had and such waving gold hair!

From *Caroling Dusk*, ed. Countée Cullen (1927)

Fantasy

GWENDOLYN B. BENNETT

I sailed in my dreams to the Land of Night
Where you were the dusk-eyed queen,
And there in the pallor of moon-veiled light
The loveliest things were seen . . .

A slim-necked peacock sauntered there
In a garden of lavender hues,
And you were strange with your purple hair
As you sat in your amethyst chair
With your feet in your hyacinth shoes.

Oh, the moon gave a bluish light
Through the trees in the land of dreams and night.
I stood behind a bush of yellow-green
And whistled a song to the dark-haired queen . . .

From *Caroling Dusk*, ed. Countée Cullen (1927)

Secret

GWENDOLYN B. BENNETT

I shall make a song like your hair . . .
Gold-woven with shadows green-tinged,
And I shall play with my song
As my fingers might play with your hair.
Deep in my heart
I shall play with my song of you,
Gently. . . .
I shall laugh
At its sensitive lustre . . .
I shall wrap my song in a blanket,
Blue like your eyes are blue
With tiny shots of silver.
I shall wrap it caressingly,
Tenderly. . . .
I shall sing a lullaby
To the song I have made
Of your hair and eyes . . .
And you will never know
That deep in my heart
I shelter a song of you
Secretly. . . .

From *Caroling Dusk*, ed. Countée Cullen (1927)

Hatred

GWENDOLYN B. BENNETT

I shall hate you
Like a dart of singing steel
Shot through still air
At even-tide,
Or solemnly
As pines are sober
When they stand etched
Against the sky.
Hating you shall be a game
Played with cool hands
And slim fingers.
Your heart will yearn
For the lonely splendor
Of the pine tree
While rekindled fires
In my eyes
Shall wound you like swift arrows.
Memory will lay its hands
Upon your breast
And you will understand
My hatred.

From *Opportunity* (1926); *Caroling Dusk,*
ed. Countée Cullen (1927); *The Book of American Negro Poetry,*
ed. James Weldon Johnson (1931)

Afterglow

GEORGIA DOUGLAS JOHNSON

Through you, I entered heaven and hell,
  Knew rapture and despair;
I vaulted o'er the plains of earth
  And scaled each shining stair;
Drank deep the waters of content
  And drained the cup of gall;
Was regal and was impotent,
  Was suzerain and thrall.

Now by reflection's placid pool,
  At evening's tranquil hour,
I smile across the backward way
  And pledge anew my vow:
For every glancing, golden gleam,
  I offer, gladly, pain;
And I would give a thousand worlds,
  To live it all again.

From *The Crisis* (March 1920)

To a Young Wife

GEORGIA DOUGLAS JOHNSON

I was a fool to dream that you
Might cross the bridge of years
From your soft springtime to my side
Where autumn shade appears.

I am sedate while you are wild,
Elusive like a sprite;
You dance into the sunny morn
While I approach the night.

I was a fool—the dream is done;
I know it cannot be.
Return and live those burning years . . .
And then, come back to me!

From *The Crisis* (May 1931)

I Want to Die While You Love Me

GEORGIA DOUGLAS JOHNSON

I want to die while you love me,
   While yet you hold me fair,
While laughter lies upon my lips
   And lights are in my hair.

I want to die while you love me,
   And bear to that still bed
Your kisses turbulent, unspent,
   To warm me when I'm dead.

I want to die while you love me,
   Oh, who would care to live
Till love has nothing more to ask
   And nothing more to give?

I want to die while you love me,
   And never, never see
The glory of this perfect day
   Grow dim or cease to be!

From *An Autumn Love Cycle* (1928)

A Kiss Requested

Kiss me good night
That I may know
Something of moonlight
Silvering snow,
While pines reach up
And darkly pray
Their deeply rooted
Earthy way;
Lower your lips
And let them rest
Against the anguish
Of my breast.

From *The Crisis* (October 1927)

All Things Insensible

KATHLEEN TANKERSLEY YOUNG

I envy the sleep
Of each cold stone
Where yellow moss
Is overgrown;

I envy flowers
That fall
Their last dark
Burial;

Insensible things
That do not hunger,
Roots that have died
And cannot stir;

All things, as stones
And moss and water,
All things that
Do not hunger.

From *Opportunity* (April 1930)

Hunger

KATHLEEN TANKERSLEY YOUNG

Your body is a dark wine
I lift to these trembling lips of mine.

Your body is a harsh dark bread
Broken that my hunger at last be fed.

At the end, this dreaming fantasy
Shall let my body and soul go free.

From *Opportunity* (June 1928)

Ecstasy

VIRGINIA A. HOUSTON

Even here, dwelling in chaos,
I find your charm is all-pervasive
And I remember only the ecstasy
Of soft lips covering mine,
Dragging my soul through my mouth,
The joy of strong young arms
Clinging, holding me ever closer,
The exquisite agony of holding you
In unfulfilled embrace.

From *The Crisis* (February 1929)

Dark Dreaming

DOROTHY KRUGER

Arrows of rain
Come darting through the trees,
Piercing with pain
The blackened nudities
Of forest kings,
And thoughts like fungous things.

Rain, and a fragrance curls
From leaves long felled by years;
Pain, and a dream unfurls
To scarves of chiffon fears.

I can remember, hours behind me,
Lying in the scented land,
Rain like a lover's kisses blindly
Showered on my fevered hand
And incense of burning brushwood slowly
Winding like a saraband
Through hours, a dream-like love made holy
In the templed dark woodland.

I can recall the crystal chain
The sun then strung around tree tops
And on my hands the brilliants lain,
And in my hair the sparkling drops,
The chrysolites on a butterfly
Dressed in a velvet black and white,
With wings widespread to pierce the sky,
And dead before the virgin flight.

The wind song changed then and the theme
Slackened until the brushwood smoke
Spiralled a cunning castle dream
And tore a turret in an oak.

Drink for my thirsting heart,
This echoed melody
Crescendos, then the smart
Of ending's threnody.

From *The Crisis* (July 1927)

Lines to a Nasturtium
(A Lover Muses)

ANNE SPENCER

Flame-flower, Day-torch, Mauna Loa,
I saw a daring bee, today, pause and soar
   Into your flaming heart;
Then did I hear crisp crinkled laughter
As the furies after tore him apart?
   A bird, next, small and humming,
Looked into your startled depths and fled . . .
Surely, some dread sight, and dafter
   Than human eyes as mine can see,
Set the stricken air waves drumming
   In his flight.

Day-torch, Flame-flower, cool-hot Beauty,
I cannot see, I cannot hear your fluty
Voice lure your loving swain,
But I know one other to whom you are in beauty
Born in vain;
Hair like the setting sun,
Her eyes a rising star,
Motions gracious as reeds by Babylon, bar
All your competing;
Hands like, how like, brown lilies sweet,
Cloth of gold were fair enough to touch her feet . . .
Ah, how the senses flood at my repeating,
As once in her fire-lit heart I felt the furies
Beating, beating.

From *Palms* 4 (October 1926); *Caroling Dusk*,
ed. Countée Cullen (1927)

At the Carnival

ANNE SPENCER

Gay little Girl-of-the-Diving-Tank,
I desire a name for you,
Nice, as a right glove fits;
For you—who amid the malodorous
Mechanics of this unlovely thing,
Are darling of spirit and form.
I know you—a glance, and what you are
Sits-by-the-fire in my heart.
My Limousine-Lady knows you, or
Why does the slant-envy of her eye mark
Your straight air and radiant inclusive smile?
Guilt pins a fig-leaf; Innocence is its own adorning.
The bull-necked man knows you—this first time
His itching flesh sees form divine and vibrant health,
And thinks not of his avocation.
I came incuriously—
Set on no diversion save that my mind
Might safely nurse its brood of misdeeds
In the presence of a blind crowd.
The color of life was gray.
Everywhere the setting seemed right
For my mood!
Here the sausage and garlic booth
Sent unholy incense skyward;
There a quivering female-thing
Gestured assignations, and lied
To call it dancing;
There, too, were games of chance
With chance for none;
But oh! The Girl-of-the-Tank, at last!
Gleaming Girl, how intimately pure and free
The gaze you send the crowd,
As though you know the dearth of beauty
In its sordid life.

We need you—my Limousine-Lady,
The bull-necked man, and I.
Seeing you here brave and water-clean,
Leaven for the heavy ones of earth,
I am swift to feel that what makes
The plodder glad is good; and
Whatever is good is God.
The wonder is that you are here;
I have seen the queer in queer places,
But never before a heaven-fed
Naiad of the Carnival-Tank!
Little Diver, Destiny for you,
Like as for me, is shod in silence;
Years may seep into your soul
The bacilli of the usual and the expedient;
I implore Neptune to claim his child to-day!

From *Negro Poets and Their Poems*, ed. Robert T. Kerlin (1923);
Caroling Dusk, ed. Countée Cullen (1927); *The Book of
American Negro Poetry*, ed. James Weldon Johnson (1931)

Summer Matures

HELENE JOHNSON

Summer matures. Brilliant Scorpion
Appears. The Pelican's thick pouch
Hangs heavily with perch and slugs.
The brilliant-bellied newt flashes
Its crimson crest in the white water.
In the lush meadow, by the river,
The yellow-freckled toad laughs
With a toothless gurgle at the white-necked stork
Standing asleep on one red reedy leg.
And here Pan dreams of slim stalks clean for piping,
And of a nightingale gone mad with freedom.
Come. I shall weave a bed of reeds
And willow limbs and pale nightflowers.
I shall strip the roses of their petals,
And the white down from the swan's neck.
Come. Night is here. The air is drunk
With wild grape and sweet clover.
And by the sacred fount of Aganippe,
Euterpe sings of love. Ah, the woodland creatures,
The doves in pairs, the wild sow and her shoats,
The stag searching the forest for a mate,
Know more of love than you, my callous Phaon.
The young moon is a curved white scimitar
Pierced thru the swooning night.
Sweet Phaon. With Sappho, sleep like the stars at dawn.
This night was born for love, my Phaon.
Come.

From *Opportunity* (July 1927); *Caroling Dusk*,
ed. Countée Cullen (1927)

Fulfillment

HELENE JOHNSON

To climb a hill that hungers for the sky,
  To dig my hands wrist deep in pregnant earth,
To watch a young bird, veering, learn to fly,
  To give a still, stark poem shining birth.

To hear the rain drool, dimpling, down the drain
  And splash with a wet giggle in the street,
To ramble in the twilight after supper,
  And to count the pretty faces that you meet.

To ride to town on trolleys, crowded, teeming,
  With joy and hurry and laughter and push and sweat—
Squeezed next a patent-leathered Negro dreaming
  Of a wrinkled river and a minnow net.

To buy a paper from a breathless boy,
  And read of kings and queens in foreign lands,
Hyperbole of romance and adventure,
  All for a penny the color of my hand.

To lean against a strong tree's bosom, sentient
  \ And hushed before the silent prayer it breathes,
To melt the still snow with my seething body
  And kiss the warm earth tremulous underneath.

Ah, life, to let your stabbing beauty pierce me
  And wound me like we did the studded Christ,
To grapple with you, loving you too fiercely,
  And to die bleeding—consummate with Life!

From *Caroling Dusk,*
ed. Countée Cullen (1927)

FOUR

~~~~~~~~~~~~~~~~~~~

Nature

At The Spring Dawn

ANGELINA WELD GRIMKÉ

I watched the dawn come,
    Watched the spring dawn come.
And the red sun shouldered his way up
    Through the grey, through the blue,
Through the lilac mists.
The quiet of it! The goodness of it!
    And one bird awoke, sang, whirred,
A blur of moving black against the sun,
    Sang again—afar off.
And I stretched my arms to the redness of the sun,
    Stretched to my fingertips,
        And I laughed.
Ah! It is good to be alive, good to love,
    At the dawn,
        At the spring dawn.

From *Negro Poets and Their Poems*, ed. Robert T. Kerlin (1923)

Dawn

ANGELINA WELD GRIMKÉ

Grey trees, grey skies, and not a star;
  Grey mist, grey hush;
And then, frail, exquisite, afar,
  A hermit-thrush.

From *Negro Poets and Their Poems*, ed. Robert T. Kerlin (1923)

A Winter Twilight

ANGELINA WELD GRIMKÉ

A silence slipping around like death,
Yet chased by a whisper, a sigh, a breath;
One group of trees, lean, naked, and cold,
Inking their crests 'gainst a sky green-gold;
One path that knows where the cornflowers were;
Lonely, apart, unyielding, one fir;
And over it softly leaning down,
One star that I loved ere the fields went brown.

From *Negro Poets and Their Poems*, ed. Robert T. Kerlin (1923);
Caroling Dusk, ed. Countée Cullen (1927)

Dusk

ANGELINA WELD GRIMKÉ

Twin stars through my purpling pane,
  The shriveling husk
Of a yellowing moon on the wane,
  And the dusk.

From *Opportunity* (April 1924); *Caroling Dusk*,
ed. Countée Cullen (1927)

Grass Fingers

ANGELINA WELD GRIMKÉ

Touch me, touch me,
Little, cool grass fingers,
Elusive, delicate grass fingers,
With your shy brushings;
Touch my face—
My naked arms—
My thighs—

My feet.
Is there nothing that is kind?
You need not fear me.
Soon I shall be too far beneath you
For you to reach me, even
With your tiny, timorous toes.

From *Caroling Dusk*, ed. Countéc Cullen (1927)

The Black Finger

I have just seen a most beautiful thing:
Slim and still,
Against a gold, gold sky,
A straight, black cypress
Sensitive
Exquisite
A black finger
Pointing upwards.
Why, beautiful still finger, are you black?
And why are you pointing upwards?

From *Opportunity* (November 1923); *The New Negro,*
ed. Alain Locke (1925)

Tenebris

ANGELINA WELD GRIMKÉ

There is a tree by day
That at night
Has a shadow,
A hand huge and black,
With fingers long and black.
　All through the dark,
Against the white man's house,
　In the little wind,
The black hand plucks and plucks
　At the bricks.
The bricks are the color of blood and very small.
　Is it a black hand,
　Or is it a shadow?

From *Caroling Dusk*, ed. Countée Cullen (1927)

Snow in October

ALICE DUNBAR-NELSON

Today I saw a thing of arresting poignant beauty:
A strong young tree, brave in its Autumn finery
Of scarlet and burnt umber and flame yellow,
Bending beneath a weight of early snow,
Which sheathed the north side of its slender trunk,
And spread a heavy white chilly afghan
Over its crested leaves.

Yet they thrust through, defiant, glowing,
Claiming the right to live another fortnight,
Clamoring that Indian Summer had not come,
Crying "Cheat! Cheat!" because Winter had stretched
Long chilly fingers into the brown, streaming hair
Of fleeing October.

The film of snow shrouded the proud redness of the tree,
As premature grief grays the strong head
Of a virile, red-haired man.

From *Caroling Dusk*, ed. Countée Cullen (1927)

October

ISABEL NEILL

Now gypsy fires burn bright in every tree,
Now countless vagrant birds are winging south;
The white roads beckon and, unsought, yet sweet,
Old songs of nomad days are in my mouth.

I burn with every tree, I fly with every bird,
And know some gypsy witch, with mystic skill,
Has traced her crooked pattern across my heart.

From *Opportunity* (October 1928)

Autumn

MARJORIE MARSHALL

Mellow sunlight, soothing, warm,
Ripened grains which gayly bloom on the hills,
Swaying stalks like graceful arms
There beneath the sun at noon, round and bright.

Maple leaves turned richly brown—
Save where deep blush pink is seen near the edge—
Wafted gently, softly down
To cool stones, moss-grown and green, nestled there.

Russet apples braving cold,
Sulking 'neath protecting leaves from the sun;
Burnished skins hid hearts of gold,
Such enticing loot for thieves, fit for gods!

Knoll and copse now redly tinged,
Quivering in the amber air, yield their fruit.
Autumn's almoner, the wind,
Scatters them like blessings rare on the earth.

From *The Crisis* (November 1928)

Desire

MARJORIE MARSHALL

I would be one with the morning
To hold in my throat
Soft ecstasies
Of bird notes;
And catch in my hair
Faint traceries of light
From dawn clouds.

I would be one with the evening
To clasp in my hands
Strange brilliancy
Of stardust;
And know in my soul
The loneliness of moon
And darkness.

From *The Crisis* (June 1928)

Nostalgia

MARJORIE MARSHALL

I shall go forth from here;
These burning streets shall know
My songs no more—
And I shall guard my ears
Against the rigid cry
Of steel on stone.
Each pallid dawn that comes
Shall seek in vain to wake
My tired soul;
For I have felt the kiss
Of fresh-blown winds that roam
Through silent hills,
And I have heard the call
Of things that stand and wait
Beneath the moon.

From *The Crisis* (November 1929)

December Portrait

KATHLEEN TANKERSLEY YOUNG

She now retraces her steps once more
Over the length of room to the dark window.
She stoops to the ancient piano
And fingers the white keys that pour
Strange music of remembered spring thunder
That she once heard in a youth long dead.
She has not forgotten; she turns her head
To stare into the dark, and hears the winds stir
A new sound: although now vaguely familiar
And yet altogether strange, the chords grow
Crazily wild, and the black window
Rattles, and music continues thunder.
Some way of sound her dreams may transcend
These stairways of snow, and snow, and wind.

From *Opportunity* (December 1930)

Want

MAE V. COWDERY

I want to take down with my hands
The silver stars
That grow in heaven's dark blue meadows
And bury my face in them.

I want to wrap all around me
The silver shedding of the moon
To keep me warm.

I want to sell my soul
To the wind in a song
To keep me from crying in the night.
I want to wake and find
That I have slept the day away.
Only nights are kind now . . .
With the stars . . . moon . . . winds and me. . . .

From *The Crisis* (November 1928)

Interlude

MAE V. COWDERY

I like this quiet place
Of lawns and trees well kept
And bright geometric gardens
Where droning bees hover and lift
On pollen-burdened wings . . .
Where even sunlight is genteel
And birds are shy and gently scarlet.

I love this quiet place
Of sane and placid beauty,
But soon I shall return
To be torn anew
At the bold thrust of skyscrapers
Against a murky sky
And the strident song
Of cars and people rushing by.

At times I shall remember
This quietude of lawns and trees
And shy birds swiftly scarlet . . .
This place I love but not enough
To linger overlong . . .

Life must go on . . . and with it
Interludes like this. . . .

From *We Lift Our Voices* (1936)

The Wind Blows

MAE V. COWDERY

The wind blows.
My soul is like a tree
Lifting its face to the sun,
Flinging wide its branches
To catch the falling rain,
To breathe into itself a fragrance
Of far-off fields of clover,
Of hidden vales of violets,—
The wind blows,—
It is spring!

The wind blows.
My soul is like sand,
Hot, burning sand
That drifts and drifts
Caught by the wind,
Swirling, stinging, swatting,
Silver in the moonlight.
Soft breath of lovers' feet
Lulled to sleep by the lap of waves,—
The wind blows,—
It is summer!

The wind blows.
My soul is still
In silent reverie,
Hearing sometimes a sigh
As the frost steals over the land,
Nipping everywhere.
Earth is dead.
The woods are bare.
The last leaf is gone,
Nipped by death's bitter frost.

My youth grown grey
Awaits the coming of
The new year.
The wind blows,—
It is winter!

From *Opportunity* (October 1927); *Anthology of Magazine Verse*,
ed. William S. Braithwaite (1928)

Four Poems

MAE V. COWDERY

After the Japanese

Night turned over
In her sleep
And a star fell
Into the sea.

Earth was a beautiful
Snow woman
Until the rain
Washed her face one day.

I am the rain
Throbbing futilely
On the cold roof
Of your heart.

The moon
Is a madonna
Cradling in the crescent curve
Of her breast
A newborn star.

Of Earth

A mountain
Is earth's mouth . . .
She thrusts her lovely
Sun-painted lips
Through the clouds
For heaven's kiss.

A hill is earth's soul . . .
She raises her
Verdant joyous prayer

Unto the gods
On dawn-tinged thrones.

A river
Is earth's grief . . .
Tears from the hidden wells
Of her soul . . .

O Earth . . . why do you weep?

Poplar Tree

Oftimes I wish that I could be
Like yonder rustling poplar tree,

And with green arms hold to my breast
Secrets the twittering birds confessed,

To have the winds blow thru my hands
Unsung melodies of far-off lands;

To sink my feet deep into earth
Down to the river that gave me birth,

And thrust my face into heaven's blue
To watch what all the angels do.

Oftimes I wish that I could be
Like yonder rustling poplar tree,

But for today I'm satisfied
To share spring's magic by your side.

God Is Kind

God
Is kind,
He lets us dream
Of untarnished silver . . .
Of skies that have never known

The pain of a storm . . .
Of the peace and contentment
In a robin's even'song.

We dream of love
Without its aftermath
Of loneliness. . . .

God
Is kind,
He lets us dream
Of unattainable things!

From *We Lift Our Voices* (1936)

Portraiture

ANITA SCOTT COLEMAN

Black men are the tall trees that remain
Standing in a forest after a fire.
   Flames strip their branches,
   Flames sear their limbs,
   Flames scorch their trunks.
   Yet stand these trees
   For their roots are thrust deep
   In the heart of the earth.
Black men are the tall trees that remain
Standing in a forest after a fire.

From *The Crisis* (June 1931)

Locust Trees

MARGARET L. THOMAS

No locust grows alone;
A pine tree dares to go
To almost any land.
Young willows follow brooks,
Then one waits long to die.
A maple in a meadow
Lives far from other trees;
No palm nor aloe fears solitude.
But locust trees,—
With pendant leaves,
And blossoms swaying like white tails
Of peacocks on the grass,—
No locust grows alone.
The scent of locust flowers,
Deep buried in the darkness,
Passed quick at night,
Is like the look of one
Who would speak
But cannot.

From *The Crisis* (February 1929)

My window opens out into the trees,
And in that small space
Of branches and of sky
I see the seasons pass,
Behold the tender green
Give way to darker heavier leaves.
The glory of the autumn comes
When, steeped in mellow sunlight,
The fragile, golden leaves
Against a clear blue sky
Linger in the magic of the afternoon
And then reluctantly break off
And filter down to pave
A street with gold.
Then bare, gray branches
Lift themselves against the
Cold December sky,
Sometimes weaving a web
Across the rose and dusk of late sunset,
Sometimes against a frail new moon,
And one bright star riding
A sky of that dark, living blue
Which comes before the heaviness
Of night descends, or the stars
Have powdered the heavens.
Winds beat against these trees;
The cold, but gentle rain of spring
Touches them lightly;
The summer torrents strive
To lash them into a fury
And seek to break them—
But they stand.
My live is fevered

And a restlessness at times,
An agony—again a vague
And baffling discontent
Possesses me.
I am thankful for my bit of sky
And trees, and for the shifting
Pageant of the seasons.
Such beauty lays upon the heart
A quiet.
Such eternal change and permanence
Take meaning from all turmoil
And leave serenity
Which knows no pain.

From *Opportunity* (November 1927); *Caroling Dusk,*
ed. Countée Cullen (1927)

Substitution

ANNE SPENCER

Is Life itself but many ways of thought,
Does *thinking* furl the poets' pleiades,
Is in His slightest convolution wrought
These mantled worlds and their men-freighted seas?
He thinks . . . and being comes to ardent things:
The splendor of the day-spent sun, love's birth,—
Or dreams a little, while creation swings
The circle of His mind and Time's full girth . . .
As here within this noisy peopled room
My thought leans forward . . . quick! you're lifted clear
Of brick and frame to moonlit garden bloom,—
Absurdly easy now our walking, dear,
Talking, my leaning close to touch your face . . .
His All-Mind bids us keep this sacred place!

From *Caroling Dusk*, ed. Countée Cullen (1927)

[God never planted a garden]

ANNE SPENCER

God never planted a garden
But He placed a keeper there
And the keeper ever razed the ground
And built a city where
God cannot walk at the eve of day,
Nor take the morning air.

(unpublished)

Creed

ANNE SPENCER

If my garden oak spares one bare ledge
For a boughed mistletoe to grow and wedge;
And all the wild birds this year should know
I cherish their freedom to come and go;
If a battered worthless dog, masterless, alone,
Slinks to my heels, sure of bed and bone;
And the boy just moved in, deigns a glance-assay,
Turns his pockets inside out, calls, "Come and play!"
If I should surprise in the eyes of my friend
That the deed was *my* favor he'd let me lend;
Or hear it repeated from a foe I despise,
That I whom he hated was chary of lies;
If a pilgrim stranger, fainting and poor,
Followed an urge and rapped at my door,
And my husband loves me till death puts apart,
Less as flesh unto flesh, more as heart unto heart:
I may challenge God when we meet That Day,
And He dare not be silent or send me away.

From *Caroling Dusk*, ed. Countée Cullen (1927)

[Night is like an avalanche]

BESSIE MAYLE

Night is like an avalanche
Sliding down the sky.
It covers me with black and gold
While other shades stand by.

Blackest nights show up the stars—
Stars of yellow gold;
Royal stars which prove to be
Very, very old.

White against a sheen of black
Shows the finest lines,
Showing too the falser tones
The finer ones entwine.

Background shades are ruling shades,
And for the world it's black—
You can find it in the east
And on the jungle's track.

What does it matter if white lights
Can boast their rays before—
Brightest days burn out themselves,
And night rules evermore.

From *The Crisis* (May 1930)

[Skylines]

BESSIE MAYLE

Skylines
Are marking me in today—
Like huge arms
The mountains hold my valley in,
And many an age goes by.

Huge things are jealous things—
Like mountains
Locking me in
And the world out.

Huge things are silly things—
Like mountains
Locking out the world's eye,
Forgetting all about the stars.

From *The Crisis* (May 1930)

Mattinata

EFFIE LEE NEWSOME

When I think of the hosts of little ones
Who wake to a birdless dawn,
Who know of no meadow that waits for them,
No pool with its dragonflies
All bathed with the silver of morning light
Like the lights that flash on the pool;
When I think of that trystless waking today—
So far as to meadows and meads,
So far as to tossing billows of wheat,
So far as to millet tides,
So far as to orchards and woods to seek,
To swing from the king sweet trees—
I fear that the dawn's too rich for my share,
I fear I have robbed some child
Of the fragrance of dew,
Of the birds' first notes,
Of the warm kind light from God—
All sent in tints of nasturtium blooms—
For the little red hearts of childhood.

From *The Crisis* (July 1927)

Memory

EFFIE LEE NEWSOME

I have seen the robins
Molding their nests with their bosoms—
Now I live in the town.

Yet street nor swirl of traffic
Can dim this vision fresh,
Which shines in memory
As the spruce lives, verdant,
And glows with the freshness of cress—
I have seen brisk robins
Molding their nests with their bosoms.

I have heard the orioles
Singing their gurgling songs.
Streets of the town,
My hungry heart stares past you
To the greens and greens of the spring,
And I pity the city-bred throng
That feels not the birds in its heart a-nesting,
To whom the spring brings no breath
Of building birds in maples and poplars and oaks,
And the budding orchards
That rain down the blooms and the dew

From *The Crisis* (January 1931)

Wild Roses

MARY EFFIE LEE NEWSOME

What! Roses growing in a meadow
Where all the cattle browse?
I'd think they'd fear the very shadow
Of daddy's big rough cows.

From *Caroling Dusk*, ed. Countée Cullen (1927)

Sassafras Tea

MARY EFFIE LEE NEWSOME

The sass'fras tea is red and clear
In my white china cup,
So pretty I keep peeping in
Before I drink it up.

I stir it with a silver spoon,
And sometimes I just hold
A little tea inside the spoon,
Like it was lined with gold.

It makes me hungry just to smell
The nice hot sass'fras tea,
And that's one thing I really like
That they say's good for me.

From *Caroling Dusk*, ed. Countée Cullen (1927)

After Reading Bryant's Lines to a Waterfowl

ELOISE BIBB THOMPSON

No forward soul, ambition stung,
And sunk in carnal bliss,
E'er dreamed a dream so fraught with heav'n
And gave us verse like this.

No lute attuned for flattery's ear,
Or struck by greed for gain,
E'er woke such cadences so sweet
Or played so rare a strain.

Not men, but Angels sing like this,
Lit with celestial fire,
And sweep the strings with airy touch
Of an immortal lyre.

From *Opportunity* (March 1924)

The River

ETHEL M. CAUTION

The river is a decrepit old woman
Shivering in her sombre shawl of fog.
Stray wisps of gray foam cling to her dank temples.
Now and then she mutters sitting there
Huddled like a shadow against the wall.
And I cannot tell
Whether she repents some folly of her youth
Or whether she bemoans her children
Who could not pace their restless steps
To her age-tempered tread.

From *The Crisis* (March 1930)

Theft

ESTHER POPEL

The moon
Was an old, old woman tonight,
Hurrying home;
Calling pitifully to her children,
The stars,
Begging them to go home with her
For she was afraid,
But they would not.
They only laughed
While she crept along
Huddling against the dark blue wall of the Night,
Stooping low,
Her old black hood wrapped close about her ears,
And only the pale curve of her yellow cheek,
With a tear in the hollow of it,
Showing through.
And the wind laughed too,
For he was teasing the old woman,
Pelting her with snowballs,
Filling her old eyes with flakes of them,
Making her cold.
She stumbled along, shivering,
And once she fell,
And the snow buried her;
And all her jewels
Slid from the old bag
Under her arm
And fell to earth,
And the tall trees seized them,
And hung them about their necks,
And filled their bony arms with them.
All their nakedness was covered by her jewels,
And they would not give them back to her.

The old moon-woman moaned piteously,
Hurrying home;
And the wild wind laughed at her
And her children laughed too,
And the tall trees taunted her
With their glittering plunder.

From *Opportunity* (April 1925)

Night Comes Walking

ESTHER POPEL

Night comes walking out our way
In a velvet gown.
Soft she steps to music gay,
As only lovely ladies may,
While hidden cricket pipers play
In Ardwick Towne.

And in her hair, wind-tossed and free,
A million stars are tucked away—
The glint of silver carelessly
Encrusting polished ebony—
A true coquette and bold is she,
This lady gay!

The gleam of laughter in her eyes
While low she bends o'er growing things,
Is caught by roguish fireflies
Who flit about her, fall and rise,
Like stars gone crazy in the skies,
On magic wings!

Night treads softly out our way
In her sable gown,
Holds her breath while babies pray,
Chuckles, seeing Love at play;
Then with Dawn she slips away,
In Ardwick Towne!

From *Opportunity* (August 1929)

Escape

GEORGIA DOUGLAS JOHNSON

Shadows, shadows,
Hug me round
So that I shall not be found
By sorrow;
She pursues me
Everywhere,
I can't lose her
Anywhere.

Fold me in your black
Abyss;
She will never look
In this,—
Shadows, shadows,
Hug me round
In your solitude
Profound.

From *The Crisis* (May 1925); *The New Negro,*
ed. Alain Locke (1925)

What Do I Care for Morning

HELENE JOHNSON

What do I care for morning,
For a shivering aspen tree,
For sunflowers and sumac
Opening greedily?
What do I care for morning,
For the glare of the rising sun,
For a sparrow's noisy prating,
For another day begun?
Give me the beauty of evening,
The cool consummation of night,
And the moon like a love-sick lady,
Listless and wan and white.
Give me a little valley,
Huddled beside a hill,
Like a monk in a monastery,
Safe and contented and still.
Give me the white road glistening,
A strand of the pale moon's hair,
And the tall hemlocks towering,
Dark as the moon is fair.
Oh what do I care for morning,
Naked and newly born—
Night is here, yielding and tender—
What do I care for dawn!

From *Caroling Dusk*, ed. Countée Cullen (1927)

Invocation

HELENE JOHNSON

Let me be buried in the rain
In a deep, dripping wood,
Under the warm wet breast of Earth
Where once a gnarled tree stood.
And paint a picture on my tomb
With dirt and a piece of bough
Of a girl and a boy beneath a round ripe moon
Eating of love with an eager spoon
And vowing an eager vow.
And do not keep my plot mowed smooth
And clean as a spinster's bed,
But let the weed, the flower, the tree,
Riotous, rampant, wild, and free,
Grow high above my head.

From *The Book of American Negro Poetry*,
ed. James Weldon Johnson (1931)

Trees at Night

HELENE JOHNSON

Slim sentinels
Stretching lacy arms
About a slumbrous moon;
Black quivering
Silhouettes,
Tremulous,
Stencilled on the petal
Of a bluebell;
Ink spluttered
On a robin's breast;
The jagged rent
Of mountains
Reflected in a
Stilly sleeping lake;
Fragile pinnacles
Of fairy castles;
Torn webs of shadows;
And printed 'gainst the sky—
The trembling beauty
Of an urgent pine.

From *Opportunity* (May 1925)

To an Icicle

BLANCHE TAYLOR DICKINSON

Chilled into a serenity
As rigid as your pose
You linger trustingly,
But a gutter waits for you.
Your elegance does not secure
You favors with the sun.
He is not one to pity fragileness.
He thinks all cheeks should burn
And feel how tears can run.

From *Caroling Dusk*, ed. Countée Cullen (1927)

Nocturne

GWENDOLYN B. BENNETT

This cool night is strange
Among midsummer days . . .
Far frosts are caught
In the moon's pale light,
And sounds are distant laughter
Chilled to crystal tears.

From *The Crisis* (November 1923); *The Book of American Negro Poetry*, ed. James Weldon Johnson (1931)

Quatrain 2

GWENDOLYN B. BENNETT

How strange that grass should sing—
Grass is so still a thing. . . .
And strange the swift surprise of snow,—
So soft it falls and slow.

From *The Crisis* (December 1923)

Street Lamps in Early Spring

GWENDOLYN B. BENNETT

Night wears a garment
All velvet soft, all violet blue . . .
And over her face she draws a veil
As shimmering fine as floating dew . . .
And here and there
In the black of her hair
The subtle hands of Night
Move slowly with their gem-starred light.

From *Opportunity* (May 1926)

Brief Biographies

Biographical information on these poets is patchy and hard to come by. Those that appear in anthologies frequently were described in a headnote to their poems, but those who were published in *Opportunity* and *The Crisis* were not. Information is not available on several writers who appear in this anthology.

GWENDOLYN B. BENNETT (1902–1981)

Bennett's birth in Giddings, Texas, belies her cosmopolitan upbringing in Washington, D.C., and Brooklyn. Her father was a lawyer and her mother a teacher. Raised primarily by her father after a marital separation, she went to high school in Brooklyn and attended the School of Fine Arts at Columbia University, ultimately graduating from Pratt Institute in 1924. She was then hired as an assistant professor of art at Howard University. Bennett won a fellowship to study painting in Paris in 1925, and upon her return, she resumed her duties at Howard. At this time, she became an assistant editor for *Opportunity* and also cofounded the literary journal *Fire!!* Her promising career was cut short when Howard fired her in 1927 for marrying a medical student (faculty were not allowed to be involved romantically with students). The couple moved to Florida where Bennett taught high school, and then, at her urging, to Long Island. Having abandoned her own creative work, she moved to Harlem in 1935 after the death of her husband, becoming involved with community art centers there and remarrying in 1940. In the later years of her life, she worked for a consumer union, and then retired in 1968 to Kutztown, Pennsylvania, where she and her husband ran an antiques shop until her death.

ANITA SCOTT COLEMAN (?–?)

Although she was a regular contributor of fiction and poetry to *The Crisis*, nothing is known about Coleman except that she was born in Mexico and worked as a teacher.

MAE V. COWDERY (1909–1953)

Born in Philadelphia, Mae Cowdery grew up there in a prosperous middle-class home, the only child of a caterer and a social worker. As a senior at the Philadelphia High School for Girls in 1927 (of which Jessie Fauset was an alumna), she won first prize in a poetry contest run by *The Crisis*, and that same year won the Krigwa Poetry Prize for another poem. After graduation, she came to New York to attend the Pratt Institute and frequented the cabarets of Harlem and Greenwich Village. A photograph of her published by *The Crisis* in 1927 as one of that year's prizewinners reveals a young woman of unusual beauty, style, and originality, with a bow tie, tailored jacket and short, slicked-down hair. Widely published in the late twenties, Cowdery was one of the few women in her generation to bring out a volume of her own work, *We Lift Our Voices and Other Poems* (Philadelphia: Alpress Publishers, 1936). Her poetry from the early thirties indicates she had a daughter, but no mention is made of a marriage in biographical material about her. In spite of winning honors at an early age, receiving encouragement from Langston Hughes and Alain Locke, and producing a fair amount of poetry, Cowdery nonetheless fell into complete obscurity after 1936. Critic Richard Long, who met her in the early 1950s, is said to have observed: "She seemed a bright intelligence made bored and restless by her ordinary surroundings." Mae Cowdery took her own life at the age of forty-four.

CLARISSA SCOTT DELANY (1901–1927)

Delany's father was secretary to Booker T. Washington when she was born at Tuskegee Institute in Alabama. She attended Bradford College in Massachusetts and Wellesley College from which she graduated in 1923. She was a teacher at Dunbar High School in Washington, D.C., where she was good friends with co-worker Angelina Weld Grimké. Delany died shortly after her marriage in 1926.

BLANCHE TAYLOR DICKINSON (1896–?)

An important Renaissance poet who is little known today, Dickinson was born in rural Kentucky and taught there for several years, having attended Bowling Green Academy and Simmons College. She lived in Sewickley, Pennsylvania, during the twenties.

ALICE DUNBAR-NELSON (1875–1935)

A suffragist, journalist, fiction writer, and teacher as well as a poet, Alice Dunbar-Nelson was born in New Orleans to a seamstress and a sailor in the merchant marine. She attended Straight University, Cornell, Columbia, and the University of Pennsylvania, settling for a time in Washington, D.C., during a brief marriage to Paul Laurence Dunbar, the most famous Afro-American poet of late nineteenth-century America. After leaving him, she moved to Wilmington, Delaware, and married Robert Nelson, a journalist. Together they published a newspaper, *The Wilmington Advocate*, from 1920 to 1922. A suffrage organizer for the Mid-Atlantic region, Dunbar-Nelson also was an active participant in the National Association of Colored Women (NACW). She is among the earliest of the Renaissance women to publish, producing *Violets and Other Tales* at the age of twenty in 1894 and another collection of short stories, *The Goodness of St. Rocque and Other Stories*, in 1899. Her unconventional love life, marriage, and domestic arrangements are recorded in a diary recently edited by Gloria Hull, *Give Us Each Day: The Diary of Alice Dunbar-Nelson* (New York: W. W. Norton, 1984).

JESSIE REDMON FAUSET (1882-1961)

Although born in New Jersey, Jessie Fauset grew up in Philadelphia as part of a large family. Her father was an African Methodist Episcopal minister and his profession kept the family in genteel poverty. Like Angelina Weld Grimké, she was frequently the only Black person in her classes, in both high school and college, about which she has said: "I'll never forget the agony I endured on entrance day when the white girls with whom I had played and studied . . . refused to acknowledge my greeting." Fauset was to experience racism throughout her education, being denied admission to Bryn Mawr, and then coping with her singular status at Cornell (from which she graduated Phi Beta Kappa). She earned a master's degree at the University of Pennsylvania. For a time, Fauset taught French and Latin at Dunbar High School in Washington, D.C., and then became literary editor of *The Crisis* from 1919 until 1926. She is credited with "midwifing" the Harlem Renaissance through her discovery of major poets. Her work as an editor fundamentally shaped her life, but Fauset considered herself first and foremost a writer. The publication of her novel *There Is Confusion* (1924) was hailed as a stellar achievement by intellectuals of her day. She produced three other novels about women seeking independence: *Plum Bun* (1929), *The Chinaberry Tree* (1931), and *Comedy, American Style* (1933). After leaving *The Crisis*, she returned to teaching in New York; married Herbert Harris, an insurance broker, at age forty-seven; and for many years entertained notable people in her home. Fauset was a friend of Georgia Douglas Johnson, and together they mentored a new generation of women writers as well as contributing some of the most significant literature of the Harlem Renaissance.

ANGELINA WELD GRIMKÉ (1880-1958)

Angelina Weld Grimké was born in Boston, the only child of an emancipated slave and Harvard Law School graduate, Archibald Henry Grimké, and a well-to-do white woman, Sarah Stanley, who left the marriage when Angelina was very young. The famous Grimké sisters of South Carolina, feminist abolitionists, publicly acknowledged Archibald to be their brother's son. Consequently, Angelina became acquainted with a wide circle of well-known progressives. She attended Boston Normal School of Gymnastics and then became a teacher at the prestigious Dunbar High School in Washington, D.C. Grimké wrote plays and short stories as well as poetry but ended her literary career in 1930 after the death of her father. Unmarried and quietly reserved, Grimké wrote muted poems of love to other women, which have recently been discovered by Gloria Hull, who said of her: "Grimké lived a buried life." She died in seclusion in New York City.

GLADYS MAE CASELY HAYFORD (1904–1950)

Hayford's home was the Gold Coast of Africa in Sierra Leone. Her father was one of three Black lawyers there and her mother was the daughter of a judge. Educated in England, Hayford returned to Sierra Leone and became a poet and teacher. Hayford's writings reflect a high regard for her cultural roots as a member of the Fanti tribe and a strong identification with women. In the biographical note to her poems in Countée Cullen's *Caroling Dusk*, she stated the goal of her writing as follows: "I argued [at age twenty] that the first thing to do was to imbue our own people with the idea of their own beauty, superiority, and individuality, with a love and admiration for their own country, which has been systematically suppressed. Consequently, I studied the beautiful points of Negro physique, texture of skin, beauty of hair, soft sweetness of eyes, charm of curves, so that none should think it a shame to be black, but rather a glorious adventure."

VIRGINIA A. HOUSTON (?–?)

Houston's poetry appears in a 1938 anthology, *Negro Voices*, edited by Beatrice Murphy (New York: Henry Harrison), where

she is reported to be living in Cleveland, Ohio, and working for a
social service agency.

GEORGIA DOUGLAS JOHNSON (1880–1966)

The most prolific of Renaissance women poets and the first Black
woman poet of note since nineteenth-century writer and activist
Frances Harper, Johnson published four volumes of verse: *The
Heart of a Woman* (1918), *Bronze* (1922), *An Autumn Love
Cycle* (1928); *Share My World* appeared in 1962. She was born in
Atlanta and attended Atlanta University, then the Oberlin Conservatory of Music in Ohio. Though she had aspirations of becoming a composer, she taught high school in Alabama and
Washington, D.C., before assuming a post with the federal gov-
ernment after her husband's death in 1925. A playwright, fiction
writer, songwriter, and journalist, as well as poet, Johnson provided ai important meeting-place for artists and writers at her
Saturday soirées in Washington, D.C. Her home remained a
stopping-point for forty years and she continued to write until the
end of her life.

HELENE JOHNSON (1907–?)

Born and raised in Boston, Helene Johnson attended Boston University and Columbia University. Very little is known about
Johnson although she participated extensively in New York and
Boston literary circles. She was one of the co-founders of *Fire!!*, a
radical journal begun by, among others, Langston Hughes, Zora
Neale Hurston, and Gwendolyn Bennett. She was also a member
of the Boston Quill Club, along with Waring Cuney and Dorothy West, which published the *Saturday Evening Quill* from
1928 until 1930. She appears to have arrived in New York in
1926 and left a few years later. Published in every major journal
and anthology of her day, she last appears in print in the 1934
issue of *Challenge*, a Boston journal edited by Dorothy West. As
of the 1960s, she was living in Brooklyn with her husband and
children.

(MARY) EFFIE LEE NEWSOME (1885–?)

Newsome was published extensively by *The Crisis* during the Harlem Renaissance and several of her poems appear in Countée Cullen's *Caroling Dusk* (1927). Though born in Philadelphia, she was raised in Wilberforce, Ohio, where she lived during the 1920s, married to a clergyman. She attended Wilberforce College, Oberlin College, the Philadelphia Academy of Fine Arts, and the University of Pennsylvania. She published a collection of poems for children in 1940 (*Gladiola Garden*) and was reported as still living in 1973.

ANNE SPENCER (1882–1975)

Born on a Virginia plantation, Anne Spencer spent her early childhood in Martinsville, Virginia, where her father owned a bar, until her mother fled with her to North Carolina and then to Bramwell, West Virginia, where she earned a living as cook near a mining camp. Placed in the home of a middle-class Black family there, Spencer grew up in a primarily white community. She did not go to school until age eleven, when her mother sent her to Virginia Seminary in Lynchburg, where Anne was to settle for the rest of her life with Edward Spencer, a postal worker. Residing with her mother, who took over household responsibilities, Anne was freed to pursue an intellectual life of reading, writing, and conversation with prominent activists and artists of her day while tending an impressive garden that still flourishes at 1313 Pierce Street. Spencer's mentor was James Weldon Johnson, one of the key figures of the Harlem Renaissance, who saw that her poetry got published and introduced her to well-known writers. Despite her obvious skills as a poet and her political activism, Spencer failed to publish after 1931 and never published a collection. She did not stop writing, however, and remained a vibrant, beautiful, articulate woman until her death at the age of ninety-three.

ELOISE BIBB THOMPSON (1878-1927)

A poet who established her reputation before the Renaissance, Eloise Bibb Thompson was born in New Orleans, attended Oberlin College, and obtained degrees from Howard University. She was both a teacher and settlement worker, moving to Los Angeles after her marriage in 1911 and remaining there until her death in 1927.

LUCY ARIEL WILLIAMS (1905-?)

Born in Mobile, Alabama, to a physician, Williams earned a degree in music at Fisk University in 1926 and then attended Oberlin Conservatory of Music in Ohio, becoming director of music at the North Carolina College for Negroes. Williams's poem "Northboun'" won first prize in *Opportunity*'s 1926 literary contest, and was included in anthologies well past the Renaissance era. Although she later published a volume of verse (*Shape Them into Dreams: Poems* [New York: Exposition Press, 1955]), Williams appeared in print only a few times during the 1920s.

Bibliography

Abrams, M. H., ed. *English Romantic Poets*. New York: Oxford University Press, 1975.

Adams, William, Peter Conn, and Barry Slepian, eds. *Afro-American Literature*. Boston: Houghton Mifflin, 1970.

Adoff, Arnold, ed. *The Poetry of Black America*. New York: Harper & Row, 1973.

Albertson, Chris. *Bessie*. New York: Stein & Day, 1972.

Anderson, Jervis. *This Was Harlem: A Cultural Portrait, 1900–1950*. New York: Farrar, Straus & Giroux, 1982.

Aptheker, Bettina. *Woman's Legacy: Essays on Race, Sex, and Class in American History*. Amherst: University of Massachusetts Press, 1982.

Baker, Houston. *The Journey Back: Issues in Black Literature and Criticism*. Chicago: University of Chicago Press, 1980.

Barksdale, Richard, and Keneth Kinnamon, eds. *Black Writers of America: A Comprehensive Anthology*. New York: Macmillan, 1972.

Bell, Bernard. *The Afro-American Novel and Its Tradition*. Amherst: University of Massachusetts Press, 1987.

Bone, Robert. *The Negro Novel in America*. New Haven: Yale University Press, 1965.

Bontemps, Arna, ed. *American Negro Poetry*. New York: Hill & Wang, 1963.

———, ed. *The Harlem Renaissance Remembered*. New York: Dodd, Mead & Co., 1972.

Braithwaite, William S., ed. *Anthology of Magazine Verse for 1928*. New York: Harold Vinal, 1928.

Brawley, Benjamin. *The Negro in Literature and Art in the United States*. New York: Duffield & Co., 1930.

Brown, Sterling. *Negro Poetry and Drama*. Washington, D.C.: Associates in Negro Folk Education, 1937.

———, Arthur P. Davis, and Ulysses Lee, eds. New York: Citadel Press, 1941.

Butcher, Margaret Just. *The Negro in American Culture*. New York: Alfred A. Knopf, 1973.

Calverton, V. F., ed. *Anthology of American Negro Literature*. New York: The Modern Library, 1929.

Christian, Barbara. *Black Women Novelists: The Development of a Tradition, 1892–1976*. Westport, CT: Greenwood Press, 1980.

Cooke, Michael. *Afro-American Literature in the Twentieth Century*. New Haven: Yale University Press, 1984.

Cooper, Wayne. "Claude McKay and the New Negro of the 1920's." In *The Black American Writer*, Vol. 2, edited by C. W. E. Bigsby. DeLand, FL: Everett/Edwards, 1969.

Cowdery, Mae V. *We Lift Our Voices and Other Poems*. Philadelphia: Alpress Publishers, 1936.

Cripps, Thomas. *Slow Fade to Black: The Negro in American Film, 1900–1942*. New York: Oxford University Press, 1977.

Cullen, Countée, ed. *Caroling Dusk: An Anthology of Verse by Negro Poets*. 1927. Reprint. New York: Harper & Row, 1955.

Davis, Arthur P. *From the Dark Tower: Afro-American Writers, 1900–1960*. Washington, D.C.: Howard University Press, 1974.

———, and Michael Peplow, eds. *The New Negro Renaissance: An Anthology*. New York: Harper & Row, 1975.

———, and J. Saunders Redding, eds. *Cavalcade: Negro American Writing from 1760 to the Present*. Boston: Houghton Mifflin, 1971.

Faderman, Lillian. *Surpassing the Love of Men: Romantic Friendship and Love between Women from the Renaissance to the Present*. New York: William Morrow & Co., 1981.

Fauset, Jessie. *Plum Bun*. 1928. Reprint. London: Pandora Press, 1985.

Garber, Eric. "Gladys Bentley: The Bulldagger Who Sang the Blues." *Outlook* 1 (Spring 1988):52–61.

Gayle, Addison Jr., ed. *Black Expression: Essays By and About*

Black Americans in the Creative Arts. New York: Weybright & Talley, 1969.

———. *The Way of the New World: The Black Novel in America*. Garden City, NY: Anchor Books, 1975.

Giddings, Paula. *When and Where I Enter: The Impact of Black Women on Race and Sex in America*. New York: William Morrow & Co., 1984.

Govan, Sandra. "Gwendolyn Bennett: Portrait of an Artist Lost." Ph.D. dissertation, Emory University, 1980.

Greene, J. Lee. *Time's Unfading Garden: Anne Spencer's Life and Poetry*. Baton Rouge: Louisiana State University Press, 1977.

Harley, Sharon, and Rosalyn Terborg-Penn, eds. *The Afro-American Woman: Struggles and Images*. Port Washington, NY: Kinnikat Press, 1978.

Hemenway, Robert. *Zora Neale Hurston: A Literary Biography*. Urbana: University of Illinois Press, 1977.

Henri, Florette. *Black Migration: Movement North 1900–1920*. Garden City, NY: Anchor Books, 1975.

Huggins, Nathan. *The Harlem Renaissance*. New York: Oxford University Press, 1971.

———, ed. *Voices from the Harlem Renaissance*. New York: Oxford University Press, 1976.

Hughes, Langston, and Arna Bontemps, eds. *The Poetry of the Negro, 1746–1970*. Garden City, NY: Doubleday & Co., 1970.

Hull, Gloria. *Color, Sex, and Poetry: Three Women Writers of the Harlem Renaissance*. Bloomington: Indiana University Press, 1987.

———. "'Under the Days': The Buried Life and Poetry of Angelina Weld Grimké." *Conditions* 2 (Autumn 1979):17–25.

———, ed. *Give Us Each Day: The Diary of Alice Dunbar-Nelson*. New York: W. W. Norton, 1984.

Ikonné, Chidi. *From DuBois to Van Vechten: The Early New Negro Literature, 1903–1926*. Westport, CT: Greenwood Press, 1981.

———. "*Opportunity* and Black Literature, 1923–1933." *Phylon* 40 (March 1979):86–93.

Jackson, Blyden, and Louis Rubin, eds. *Black Poetry in America.* Baton Rouge: Louisiana State University Press, 1974.

Johnson, Abby Arthur. "Literary Midwife: Jessie Redmon Fauset and the Harlem Renaissance." *Phylon* 39 (June 1978): 143–153.

———, and Ronald Mayberry. *Propaganda and Aesthetics: The Literary Politics of Afro-American Magazines in the Twentieth Century.* Amherst: University of Massachusetts Press, 1979.

Johnson, Charles S., ed. *Ebony and Topaz: A Collecteanea.* 1927. Reprint. Freeport, NY: Books for Libraries Press, 1971.

Johnson, Georgia Douglas. *An Autumn Love Cycle.* 1928. Reprint. Freeport, NY: Books for Libraries Press, 1971.

———. *Bronze: A Book of Verse.* Boston: B. J. Brimmer Co., 1922.

———. *The Heart of a Woman and Other Poems.* Boston: Cornhill Publishers, 1918.

Johnson, James Weldon, ed. *The Book of American Negro Poetry.* 1931. Reprint. New York: Harcourt, Brace, and World, 1959.

Jubilee, Vincent. "Philadelphia's Afro-American Literary Circle and the Harlem Renaissance." Ph.D. dissertation, University of Pennsylvania, 1980.

Kellner, Bruce. *Carl Van Vechten and the Irreverent Decades.* Norman: University of Oklahoma Press, 1968.

———, ed. *The Harlem Renaissance: An Annotated Bibliography.* Westport, CT: Greenwood Press, 1984.

Kerlin, Robert T., ed. *Negro Poets and Their Poems.* Washington, D.C.: Associated Publishers, 1923.

Larsen, Nella. *Quicksand and Passing.* Edited by Deborah McDowell. New Brunswick: Rutgers University Press, 1986.

Lewis, David Levering. *When Harlem Was in Vogue.* New York: Alfred A. Knopf, 1981.

Lieb, Sandra. *Mother of the Blues: A Study of Ma Rainey.* Amherst: University of Massachusetts Press, 1981.

Locke, Alain, ed. *The New Negro: An Interpretation.* New York: Albert and Charles Boni, 1925.

McDowell, Deborah. "The Neglected Dimension of Jessie Fauset." In *Conjuring: Black Women, Fiction, and the Liter-*

ary Tradition, edited by Hortense Spillers and Marjorie Pryse. Bloomington: Indiana University Press, 1985.

Martin, Tony. *Literary Garveyism: Garvey, Black Arts, and the Harlem Renaissance*. Dover, MA: The Majority Press, 1983.

May, Henry F. *The End of American Innocence: A Study of the First Years of Our Time, 1912–1917*. New York: Alfred A. Knopf, 1959.

Meier, August, and Eliott Rudwick. *From Plantation to Ghetto: An Interpretive History of American Negroes*. New York: Hill & Wang, 1966.

Moore, Gerald. "Poetry in the Harlem Renaissance." In *The Black American Writer*, Vol. 2, edited by C. W. E. Bigsby. DeLand, FL: Everett/Edwards, 1969.

Murphy, Beatrice, ed. *Negro Voices*. New York: Henry Harrison Press, 1938.

Osofsky, Gilbert. *Harlem: The Making of a Ghetto, Negro New York 1890–1930*. New York: Harper & Row, 1963.

Patterson, Lindsay, ed. *A Rock Against the Wind: Black Love Poems*. New York: Dodd, Mead & Co., 1973.

Perry, Margaret. *Silence to the Drums: A Survey of the Literature of the Harlem Renaissance*. Westport, CT: Greenwood Press, 1976.

Primeau, Ronald. "Frank Horne and the Second Echelon Poets of the Harlem Renaissance." In *The Harlem Renaissance Remembered*, edited by Arna Bontemps. New York: Dodd, Mead & Co., 1972.

Redding, J. Saunders. *To Make a Poet Black*. Chapel Hill: University of North Carolina Press, 1939.

————. "The New Negro Poet in the Twenties." In *Modern Black Poets*, edited by Donald Gibson. Englewood Cliffs, NJ: Prentice-Hall, 1973.

Robinson, William, ed. *Early Black American Poets*. Dubuque, IA: William C. Brown, 1969.

Sherman, Joan, ed. *Invisible Poets: Afro-Americans and the Nineteenth Century*. Urbana: University of Illinois Press, 1974.

Shockley, Ann Allen, ed. *Afro-American Women Writers, 1746–*

1933: *An Anthology and Critical Guide*. Boston: G. K. Hall, 1988.

Singh, Amritjit. *The Novels of the Harlem Renaissance*. University Park: Pennsylvania State University Press, 1976.

Singleton, Gregory Holmes. "Birth, Rebirth, and the 'New Negro' of the 1920's." *Phylon* 3 (March 1982): 29–45.

Stetson, Erlene. "Black Feminism in Indiana, 1893–1933." *Phylon* 44 (December 1983): 292–298.

———, ed. *Black Sister: Poetry by Black American Women, 1746–1980*. Bloomington: Indiana University Press, 1981.

Sylvander, Carolyn. *Jessie Redmon Fauset, Black American Writer*. Troy, NY: The Whitston Publishing Co., 1981.

Terborg-Penn, Rosalyn. "Discrimination against Afro-American Women in the Women's Movement, 1830–1920." In *The Afro-American Woman: Struggles and Images*, edited by Sharon Harley and Rosalyn Terborg-Penn. Port Washington, NY: Kennikat Press, 1978.

Thurman, Wallace. "Negro Poets and Their Poetry." In *Black Expression: Essays By and About Black Americans in the Creative Arts*, edited by Addison Gayle, Jr. New York: Weybright & Talley, 1969.

Wagner, Jean. *Black Poets of the United States*. Urbana: University of Illinois Press, 1973.

White, Newman, and Walter Jackson, eds. *An Anthology of Verse by American Negroes*. Durham, NC: Trinity College Press, 1924.